Faces of Exploration

Encounters with 50 Extraordinary Pioneers

First published in hardback in Great Britain in 2006 by

Wigwam Press Ltd, 204 Latimer Road, London, W10 6QY

Published in association with André Deutsch, an imprint of the Carlton Publishing Group

Book design by Zain Al-Fikri Bador of Resolution Creative Ltd.

Printed by Imago Publishing Ltd, Thame, Oxfordshire.

A CIP catalogue record for this title is available from the British Library.

ISBN-10: 0 233 00199 9

ISBN-13: 978 0 233 00199 9

With grateful acknowledgement to Alex Foley and Associates Ltd.

Faces of Exploration

Encounters with 50 Extraordinary Pioneers

Portraits and interviews by Joanna Vestey

Text by Justin Marozzi
Foreword by Dame Ellen MacArthur
Introduction by Shane and Nigel Winser

ANDRE
DEUTSCH

To my very dear children

~ Jago and Chloe

Contents

Preface

What, in the twenty-first century, constitutes exploration and who can rightly be called an explorer? There are no easy answers to these questions. In the nineteenth century the same ones echoed along the corridors of the Royal Geographical Society, causing heated debate and controversy. To this day they still do.

The men and women in this book fall under many categories. There are scientists and adventurers, pilots and climbers, sportsmen and travellers. For me, however, it is their vision, their quest for knowledge and their readiness to share their discoveries with a wider audience that makes them pioneers, explorers in their chosen field. Each of them speaks to the inquiring urge and the instinct to discover fresh horizons that lie within us all and make us human. Above all, though, *Faces of Exploration* is a personal collection.

It was through my association with the Royal Geographical Society and the Explorers Club that I began to meet these remarkable people and first conceived of this project. It was important to me to focus on the contemporary, rather than historic, field of exploration. These are men and women whose interests range from mountains and poles to jungles, deserts, oceans and beyond, into the frozen mystery of space. Their record in the field makes a lie of the often repeated claim that true exploration has been and gone. In fact, it is, as these pioneers amply demonstrate, alive and well.

Faces of Exploration has been three wonderful years in the making. Explorers are restless types and tracking them down has been a challenge. Outside the UK, I have travelled to the US, Norway, Monte Carlo, Italy, Switzerland, France and Russia in my quest to portray them as they are in everyday life, in various settings: at home, on boats and roof terraces, in five-star hotels and auditoriums, even on mountains. I am grateful for the time they have each so generously spared and for their unanimous support and belief in this project.

On a personal level I have found these men and women truly inspirational. They have had the courage to pursue their dreams against the odds. It is my hope that their stories and extraordinary achievements will be an abiding inspiration to every reader.

Joanna Vestey

There are two moments in my life which led me to where I am today. The first was when I sailed for the very first time. I was only four years old but I can still remember it vividly. I remember the feeling of total freedom on the water, the heightened sense of opportunity and adventure – at that age, I knew a boat could take you anywhere in the world. It was a feeling that I had never experienced before and it was not long before everything in my life was about sailing, I lived and breathed it.

The second moment was at seventeen whilst studying for my A levels. I always thought I would go to university and I had a strong inclination to become a vet as I loved animals and I never realised that sailing could actually be a career, even though sailing and spending time fixing boats took up the majority of my spare time and was my real passion. I was studying hard but contracted glandular fever just before my A levels and was ill for the next month. I was completely laid up, I had absolutely no energy and felt terrible. It was during this illness that I watched a video about the Whitbread Round the World Race – a crewed race around the world with stops and for 'professional' sailors. Watching this was a revelation for me, as I realised for the first time that sailing could give me a career. As it was, I had fallen behind in my studies and was unable to gain the grades I needed to train to be a vet. That was the catalyst for what followed, as I decided to follow my heart and to make sailing my life, and since that moment I haven't turned back.

It has been an amazing journey so far, one that began a long time ago, and one I hope will continue for a while yet. I am also incredibly fortunate with my 'journey' and I am in the company of some amazing people – the team behind the scenes who make the sailing possible, my family and friends who support me all the way. With passion, drive, hard work and unflinching support, you soon realise that anything is possible.

For me, this remarkable collection of men and women have shown that no matter how great the odds are stacked against you, it is possible to achieve what to many may seem the impossible. Without these people, we would never progress, or break into new territory, and above all, we would never inspire the next generation to follow in our footsteps…

Ellen MacArthur

Introduction

The first ascent of Mount Everest without oxygen

Mapping of the deep oceanic ridge of the mid-Atlantic with sonar

Using tower cranes to explore the rainforest canopy

Crossing Antarctica alone on skis and without dogs

Cave-diving in the Blue Holes of the Bahamas

The fastest circumnavigation of the globe by balloon

Images from space showing the earth rise over the moon

These are just a few of the milestones of exploration that we have had the privilege to witness over thirty years spent at the Royal Geographical Society, latterly running its Expedition Advisory Centre. On every Monday during the academic year, extraordinary people stand on the stage at the Royal Geographical Society to share their experiences with the audience of Fellows and members. Only a handful of these remarkable men and women are prepared to describe themselves as explorers in the tradition of Livingstone and Stanley, Scott and Shackleton but each speaker introduces those present to new places and new ideas from their own personal experiences.

Like those who have been chosen to appear in this book, they have taken a less conventional path in life. Highly motivated, often obsessive, they are driven to better understand the world and even the physical limitations of human endeavour. When Tenzing Norgay and Ed Hillary stood on top of Mount Everest in 1953 there were doubts that anyone could survive at that altitude, and even 25 years later Reinhold Messner and Peter Habler's climb of Everest without supplementary oxygen was greeted with astonishment by the mountaineering community. This was 'pushing the limits' in some of the harshest conditions on earth.

It was no coincidence that the last continent to be explored was Antarctica, and that period of exploration in the early part of the twentieth century was known as the Heroic Age. Ranulph Fiennes and Robert Swan have nothing but admiration for their illustrious predecessors, particularly Captain Robert Falcon Scott and his compatriots, who died in appalling circumstances in their attempt to better understand this frozen land. And the public continue to admire those who strive to cross the polar wastes: Wally Herbert's trans-Arctic crossing remains unrivalled, and Borge Ousland's solo crossing of Antarctica is an extraordinary feat. Anyone with doubts about how remote you are in Antarctica, even with modern communication methods, should read the stories of Jerri Nielsen and Steve Brooks.

Only the power of the world's oceans seems to throw out equivalent great physical challenges. Challenges willingly met and overcome by today's great yachtsmen and women, epitomised by Chay Blyth, and Ellen MacArthur, and much admired by the public nearly five hundred years after the completion of Magellan's first circumnavigation of the globe in 1522.

Modern advances in technology have given us new forms of transport: Betrand Piccard and Steve Fossett have piloted balloons around the world, an activity also taken up by polar traveller David Hempleman-Adams. Bear Grylls, in addition to climbing Everest, crossed the Atlantic in a rigid inflatable boat. While Story Musgrave has had the opportunity to venture into space, and Buzz Aldrin the extraordinary experience of walking on the moon.

In the nineteenth century the tropical forests of the world were as little known as space is today. Returning explorers were sought out with as much thirst for knowledge as astronauts were in the 1960s. This is the time when John Hemming and Robin Hanbury-Tenison were travelling, by river, deep into the Amazon jungle. They were so horrified by the plight of the native South American Indians that they were inspired to found Survival International, now the leading organisation fighting for the rights of indigenous peoples worldwide. Christina Dodwell and Benedict Allen have also found fascination in the world's tropical forests and been dependent on local people on their travels.

Those wishing to better understand the biodiversity of the tropics are looking high into the forest canopy. The high trees of tropical forests are being explored using innovative techniques such as tower cranes, with their long arms extending over the tree tops, and inflatable rafts floating on the tree crowns. By these means, biologist Andrew Mitchell is able to reach and study the unique and little known plants and animals that live there.

New discoveries in scientific exploration are coming thick and fast. To quote John Hemming, this is the 'Golden Age of Exploration'. George Schaller and Jane Goodall have significantly changed our understanding of the natural world and championed biological conservation for several decades. While Michael Novacek has helped us better understand the creatures who inhabited earth before humankind.

Today the frontiers of exploration, apart from space, are the caves deep within the earth and underwater in the deep oceans. The only speleologist to be profiled here is Andy Eavis, who has spent a lifetime exploring, surveying and mapping some of the world's largest and most extensive cave systems in Borneo and China, where there is still much to do. But it is the deep oceans where the explorers of the twenty-first century are going to make their biggest discoveries. Marie Tharp was the cartographer on the Lamont-Doherty Earth Observation team that first mapped the Mid-Atlantic Ridge, which gave credence to the theory of plate tectonics. Bob Ballard used deep-sea submersibles to document entirely new life forms around sub-sea hydrothermal vents. While Jean-Michael Cousteau continues his father's legacy campaigning for the protection of the seas using modern communication methods such as documentary film-making and the Internet.

The role of the explorer as communicator should never be underestimated. It is that ability to tell the story that can change people's understanding of the world. Many of those mentioned above are superb communicators. Bob Ballard, for example, has brought real-time exploration into school rooms worldwide, enabling children to share in the excitement of discovery. This is an idea Oliver Steeds shares passionately. The great desert explorer Wilfred Thesiger will long be remembered as both an outstanding travel writer and photographer, whose empathy for the people he travelled with pours out of every page. Other travel writers such as Dervla Murphy and Heinrich Harrer have opened up whole new worlds to their readers.

These are just some of the fifty pioneers who have inspired RGS Fellows, Joanna Vestey and Justin Marozzi. Justin's wonderfully engaging text puts their explorations into context and through their first-hand quotes gives a remarkable insight into what motivates them and how they view their own achievements. Joanna, the driving force behind this book, is a photographer, pilot and traveller herself who has brought together a stunning body of work – black and white portraits that let us look into the faces and possibly the souls of these fascinating men and women. Enjoy – we truly hope that you too will be inspired to go out and see the world for yourself and then in your own way make a difference.

Shane and Nigel Winser
Oxfordshire, February 2006

The Explorers

Sir EDMUND HILLARY

At 11.30am on 29 May 1953, a lanky beekeeper from Auckland stepped onto the summit of Mount Everest and into the legend books. Together with the Nepalese Sherpa Tenzing Norgay, Edmund Hillary was the first to set foot on the summit of the world's highest mountain – 29,028 feet above sea level – a feat which had eluded seven major expeditions between 1920 and 1952.

It was auspicious timing for the British Everest Expedition. In clipped English accents the BBC announced news of the success on the eve of Queen Elizabeth's coronation, delighting a nation still weary from war and the austerity of the early 1950s.

Recalling the details of the epic climb for *National Geographic* magazine in 1954, Hillary summarised the excitement and relief of the last moments.

"I cut my way cautiously up the next few feet, probing ahead with my pick. The snow is solid, firmly packed. We stagger up the final stretch. We are there. Nothing above us, a world below. I feel no great elation at first, just relief and a sense of wonder. Then I turn to Tenzing and shake his hand. Even through the snow glasses, the ice-encrusted mask, the knitted helmet, I can see that happy, flashing smile. He throws his arms around my shoulders, and we thump each other, and there is very little we can say or need to say."

Once they had completed the treacherous route down from the summit, Hillary's reaction was more prosaic. "We've knocked the bastard off!" he famously told George Lowe, a fellow New Zealander on the expedition. His life would never be the same again. Knighted by the Queen, he became world-famous. With

Sir John Hunt, the expedition's leader, he co-authored *The Ascent of Everest*, an instant bestseller. To this day, all Everest climbers who approach the summit from the south must first negotiate the Hillary Step, a forty-foot ice-covered rock step named in his honour.

It is easy now, more than half a century after that legendary ascent, to forget how much uncertainty then surrounded man's ability to deal with such extreme altitudes.

"We didn't know if it was humanly possible to reach the top of Mount Everest, and even using oxygen as we were, if we did get to the top, we weren't at all sure whether we wouldn't drop dead or something of that nature."

Hillary was born in 1919 and grew up in Auckland. As a child he was something of a dreamer, who did not have many friends. "I was a very keen walker and, as I walked along the roads and tracks around this countryside area, I'd be dreaming. My mind would be miles away and I would be slashing villains with swords and capturing beautiful maidens and doing all sorts of heroic things, just purely in my dreams. I used to love to walk for hours and hours and my mind would be far away in all sorts of heroic efforts." At 16, he made his first visit to the mountains and fell in love with the snow and ice. "It changed my life," he says. He went on to start climbing seriously, first in his own country, then in the Alps and later still in the Himalayas, where he demonstrated his prowess and suitability for the attempt on Everest by climbing 11 peaks of 20,000 feet or more.

In 1951-1952, Hillary threw down another marker on two Everest reconnaissance expeditions which brought him to the attention of Colonel John Hunt, leader of the 1953 expedition co-sponsored by the Joint Himalayan Committee of the Alpine Club of Great Britain and the Royal Geographical Society. A Swiss expedition had turned back 1,000 feet from the summit in 1952 so all knew it was make or break for Hunt's team. Together, they seized the opportunity.

For a man whose childhood hero was the British explorer Sir Ernest Shackleton, who described Apsley Cherry-Garrard's classic book *The Worst Journey in the World* as his 'bible', it was fitting that Hillary should turn from climbing mountains to traversing the Antarctic. Between 1955–1958, he led the New Zealand section of the trans-Antarctic expedition and reached the South Pole by tractor. Though the exploration continued – in 1977, he led a jet-boat expedition to the mountain source of the River Ganges – increasingly it took second place to improving the welfare of the Nepalese. Above all, he threw himself into providing the Sherpas with airfields, schools, hospitals and medical clinics. It was his way of thanking them for Tenzing's help in getting him to the top of the world.

Personal tragedy intervened in 1975, when his wife and youngest daughter, flying into the hills of Nepal where he was working on a hospital, were killed in a plane crash. It was "an absolute

disaster", he said later. "The two people that meant most to me in life had been killed in one fell swoop." Solace was slow to arrive and came only with his remarriage to June, a family friend, years later.

Friends and colleagues describe Hillary as a modest man, never one to brag or boast about his achievements. As he told one interviewer with typical understatement: "In many ways, I'm basically a very mediocre person."

With full-blown exploration behind him, the scope of Hillary's interests and activities broadened. He has worked on medical and conservation campaigns for, among others, UNICEF and the WWF and founded the Himalaya Trust. Whatever his protestations to the contrary, the rest of the world will remember him in grand, heroic terms.

As the Duke of Edinburgh, patron of the 1953 expedition, wrote in the foreword to *Ascent of Everest*: "In the human terms of physical effort and endurance alone it will live in history as a shining example to all mankind."

Hillary's own message to future generations is typically pithy. He is not a man given to extended monologues. He says:

"Aim high! There is little virtue in easy victory."

"I think motivation is the single most important factor in any sort of success. Physical fitness is important, technical skill is important, and maybe even the desire for money is important in some respects. But a sort of basic motivation, the desire to succeed, to stretch yourself to the utmost, is the most important factor. Certainly in the field of exploration, it's the thing that makes the difference between someone who does really well and someone who doesn't."

Sir Edmund Hillary

Lowe on wireless radio – with Hillary enjoying the conversation, 1953.

BERTRAND PICCARD

If anyone ever wanted to prove that exploration ran in the genes, their first port of call would probably be the Piccard family. Bertrand Piccard's grandfather Auguste Piccard invented the pressurised cockpit, enabling balloons, aeroplanes and rockets to fly as high as 50,000 feet.

He was the inspiration for Hergé's Professor Calculus in the Tintin series. Auguste also invented the first bathyscaphe, a deep-sea submersible which enabled his son Jacques to complete the world's deepest submarine dive of 10,916 metres along the Marianas Trench in the Pacific. The illustrious bloodline meant the young Bertrand enjoyed an enviable access to a number of his explorer idols.

"Thanks to the achievements of my father and grandfather, as a child I was able to meet most of my heroes, like Charles Lindbergh, Werner von Braun, and several astronauts from the American space programme," he says. "The highlights were certainly the launches of *Apollo 7* to *Apollo 12* that I was able to attend with my parents as guests of NASA."

"From that moment, it seemed to me that life would only be interesting if you explored it, if you could escape the rut of everyday routine and commit yourself to impossible targets."

Born in Lausanne in 1958, Piccard took to the air as a 16-year-old with his discovery of hang-gliding and microlighting, sports in which he was to become a pioneer in Europe. Among his achievements in this field, he was European hang-glider aerobatics champion in 1985 and also held a world altitude record for a time.

If exploration of the skies and seas runs in the family, so does science. Piccard studied to become a doctor and subsequently specialised in psychiatry and psychotherapy. His natural curiosity led to him to the study of hypnosis, together with Eastern, particularly Taoist, traditions.

Piccard's skills as a psychiatrist and hypnotist were in demand in 1992, the year he returned to the family tradition of ballooning. The Belgian Wim Verstraeten, an entrant in the 1992 Chrysler Challenge, the first transatlantic balloon race, reckoned Piccard would make an ideal co-pilot. It was an inspired choice. They won the 5,000 kilometre race in five days.

This high-altitude experience kindled Piccard's ballooning spirit. His ambition was simple: to fly around the world non-stop, borne only on currents of wind. It was the last great prize in aviation and it became the last great adventure of the twentieth century. He approached the Swiss watchmakers Breitling with his idea and in 1997, after three years preparing for the round-the-world flight, took off in *Breitling Orbiter 1*. This attempt and the second – which established a record for the longest flight in terms of duration – were both aborted. At this point he wondered whether he should continue trying.

A timely gift from Jean-Jules Verne, grandson of Jules, gave him the belief he needed. It was Guy de Maupassant's *Une Vie*, a leather-bound book which had once belonged to Jules Verne. "It came at a moment when I was racked by doubts... about the flight, about the wisdom of the whole enterprise," Piccard recalled in his book *Around the World in 20 Days*. "When I opened my heart to the founder of the Jules Verne Adventure Association asking whether he thought that I was right to risk so much – my family, my job, my nice life – he gave me a robust answer. 'It's not a question of whether or not you have the right to fly,' he said. 'You have a duty. Mankind needs people to do things like this. People are going to dream with you. The fact that we are giving you this unique book shows how much we trust you.' I found his words very moving and returned to Switzerland with my energy restored, suddenly seeing everything clearly. In other words, that book was one of the crucial factors that got *Orbiter 3* into the air and me out of an ocean of doubt in which I was drowning."

The rest, as they say, was (ballooning and aviation) history. On 21 March 1999, cocooned in their capsule beneath the towering balloon that was as high as the Tower of Pisa and weighed as much as a fighter jet, Piccard and his British co-pilot Brian Jones touched down in Egypt after a 45,755 kilometres flight lasting 19 days, 21 hours and 47 minutes. Their pioneering round-the-world flight broke seven records. It was the longest in aviation history, both in duration and distance.

Not surprisingly, the successful landing in Egypt was the greatest moment of Piccard's career. "Equally moving was the moment when I first saw the capsule of the *Breitling Orbiter 3* in the Milestone Hall of Flight of the Smithsonian Air and Space Museum in Washington, next to the Spirit of St. Louis and the *Apollo 11* capsule in front of which, as a child, I had dreamed of exploration."

On completing their stunning journey, Piccard and Jones received a string of awards and accolades from, among other organisations, the Fédération Aéronautique Internationale, the National Geographic Society, the Explorers Club and the American Academy of Achievement. Piccard was also awarded the coveted Légion d'Honneur. Dedicating their achievement to the children of the world, Piccard and Jones established the Winds of Hope Foundation, an organisation dedicated to raising awareness of some of the world's worst humanitarian problems.

A goodwill Ambassador for the United Nations Population Fund, Piccard the scientist and adventurer is also something of a philosopher on the motivational speaking circuit. "Hot-air ballooning is for me a metaphor for life," he explains.

"Just as a hot-air balloon is a prisoner of the currents which propel it, people are captive to their problems and destiny."

"I believe strongly that just as a balloon can change altitude in order to find the currents which make it change direction, men and women can raise themselves up and be responsible for the direction their lives take."

Bertrand Piccard

Breitling Orbiter 3 *over the Alps just after take-off from Château-d'Oex, Switzerland, 1 March 1999.*

SYLVIA EARLE

Best known as 'Her Deepness', sometimes even the 'Sturgeon General', the marine botanist and oceanographer Sylvia Earle has been obsessed with the sea ever since she can remember. Her first experience with it came when she was swept off her feet by a wave as a three-year-old. She says she has loved it ever since.

Earle, who was born in 1935, grew up on a small farm in New Jersey and as a child always loved being taken to the coast. "They say that in some countries such as Peru, they worship the sun because they only see it when the fog breaks, and they see the sun," she told the American Academy of Achievement. "I didn't exactly worship the ocean, but I really regarded it as a very special opportunity. I can remember, as we travelled across the pine barrens and came to the sand dunes along the shore, before we could see or hear the ocean, we could smell it. And then hear it. And then finally, there it was, this great incredible expanse. And I can still feel that leap of enthusiasm, and real joy, at the prospect of finally getting out to the beach, and running around."

She was fascinated with the marine life she found there, particularly the big horse-shoe crabs with which she played, learning that if she treated them with gentleness they were unlikely to hurt her. At home, when she was not exploring the hills and woods, her nose was buried in an encyclopaedia, ferreting out new discoveries with the hunger of a would-be explorer or racing through stories by the explorer William Beebe.

When she was 12, her parents moved from New Jersey to Dunedin, Florida. Schooled at nearby Clearwater on the Gulf of Mexico, her back yard suddenly changed from a farm to the sea. Enter the world of salt marshes, sea grass beds, sea horses, urchins and more crabs. Nature revealed itself to her as endlessly fascinating and it was at this time she determined on a life involved with wild animals, little knowing she would become the world's best-known woman marine scientist.

At 18, she made her first scuba dive, shortly after winning a scholarship to Florida State University. Her major professor Harold Humm inspired her to concentrate on marine plants and has remained a life-long friend. Once one understood them, one gained a powerful insight into the ecosystem dependent upon them.

"When I was still an undergraduate student at Florida State University, I began my lifetime project with that as a starting point. I am still working on it, and expect to continue working on it. If I had ten lifetimes, I'd still be working on that same project, I'm sure... There are plants growing where people didn't expect to find plants. That leads to a whole host of questions. Why is this so? Why do they occur here? Why don't they occur somewhere else? Who eats them? Are they there throughout the whole year? How far do they range? You never run out of questions to ask."

Earle's advanced studies took her to Duke University, where she earned a Masters and subsequently, after getting married and starting a family, a PhD in 1966. Her dissertation itself – "Phaeophyta of the Eastern Gulf of Mexico" – was something of a landmark in the briny corridors of the oceanographic community, a first-hand study of unprecedented length and detail on aquatic plant life. She was simply hooked on marine exploration.

A stint at Harvard as a research Fellow was followed by the resident directorship at Cape Haze Marine Laboratory in Florida. Then, in 1968, when she was four months pregnant, Earle boarded the *Deep Diver* submersible and travelled 100 feet below the surface of the water in the Bahamas.

It was in 1970, however, that she shot to fame after leading the first team of women to live underwater for two weeks in a purpose-built laboratory off the US Virgin Islands. The Tektite Project was an experiment co-sponsored by NASA, the US Navy and the Department of the Interior to study the effects of long-term isolation. Earle was initially rejected for the first mission by authorities appalled at the prospect of men and women cohabiting underwater. It led to the all-women Tektite II expedition. The women were inevitably dubbed 'aquababes' and Earle, who was photogenic to say the least, was able to use the resulting publicity to campaign vigorously against overfishing and marine pollution.

She earned the affectionate epithet 'Her Deepness' in 1979, after a record-breaking dive which saw her walk untethered on the seabed in a pressurised one-atmosphere diving suit, 1,250 feet below the surface, a record which stands to this day. She then spent two and a half hours exploring the depths and encountering sharks, crabs and sea rays. This ground-breaking episode was recounted in *Exploring the Deep Frontier*, published in 1980. She established another record with a solo descent down to 3,000 feet in *Deep Rover*.

Teaming up with the film-maker Al Giddings, Earle made the documentary film *Gentle Giants of the Pacific*, following the great humpback whales from Hawaii to New Zealand, Australia, South Africa, Bermuda and Alaska.

The 1980s saw her entrepreneurial side unleashed with the founding of Deep Ocean Engineering and Deep Ocean Technologies with Graham Hawkes, the engineer who became her third husband. The companies design and build deep-sea submersibles at the cutting edge of technology, allowing greater penetration of the depths.

In 1990, she was appointed chief scientist for the US National Oceanic and Atmospheric Administration. The author of more than 125 scientific and popular articles and a number of books, Earle has also clocked up more than 6,000 hours underwater on over 50 expeditions. At 70, she remains a tireless campaigner for marine conservation and is an Explorer-in-Residence at the National Geographic Society and the executive director of Global Marine Programs for Conservation International, together with a number of other senior roles in the business and NGO sectors. If she had a statue for every award she had won, her house would be crammed with them.

"Wilderness is not just valuable because it's beautiful, or aesthetically appealing, it is the stabilising part of the planet that creates the good health that we have always taken for granted. Most of the sea is still in this healthy, wilderness state. But at an alarming rate, we are changing the oceans."

"When I go down in the ocean there may be a lot of unknowns,
but I feel comfortable about the risks."

Sylvia Earle

Sylvia Earle floats outside the Deep Rover submersible, the research vessel she helped develop. It is
piloted by her stepdaughter, Melanie Hawks.

BUZZ ALDRIN

*On 20 July 1969, watched by the largest worldwide television audience in history, two men walked out of the **Eagle Lander** spacecraft and stepped onto the moon for the first time. The words of one of them became legendary. "That's one small step for man, one giant leap for mankind," said Neil Armstrong, epitomising the insatiable human quest to explore new frontiers.*

Armstrong's less immediately celebrated colleague on the *Apollo XI* mission, the man who was second to set foot on another planet, was Buzz Aldrin. His words on stepping onto the level Sea of Tranquillity, beamed back to Houston, were, "Beautiful, beautiful. Magnificent desolation."

As if to make up for beating him to the record books, Armstrong, whose job it was to record the moonwalk, captured Aldrin on film in the iconic shot of an astronaut with the *Eagle Lander* reflected in his visor, a triumphant picture recalling the famous image of Sherpa Tenzing on the summit of Everest. It was an epic milestone in the history of exploration. Aldrin remembers of that day:

> *"I think the most exhilarating moment for me will always be the moment of exact touchdown on the surface of the moon when the engine was shut off and the spacecraft settled into the lunar dust."*

The two men spent two hours fifteen minutes exploring the moon's surface, collecting 21 kilograms of soil samples, conducting a series of experiments and taking photos. They found time also to plant the American flag and unveil a plaque which said:

> "Here men from planet earth
> First set foot upon the moon
> July 1969, A.D.
> We came in peace for all mankind."

Messages of congratulation flooded in from around the world. The Pope called it "a celebration on the part of the whole terrestrial globe, with no more unsurpassable bounds of human existence, but openness to the expanse of endless space and a new destiny." Watching the live broadcast, President Nixon described the landing as "one of the greatest moments of our time." The last 22 seconds of the descent were the longest he had ever lived through, he said.

Born in New Jersey in 1930, Aldrin was a gifted student whose father, Edwin Eugene Aldrin, was an aviation pioneer who worked in rocket development. Buzz's enigmatic nickname came early on. Had it not been for his baby sister's inability to pronounce the word 'brother' – her version was 'Buzzer' – he would probably never have earned it (he legally changed his name to Buzz in 1988).

Graduating from West Point in 1951, third in his class, he was in time to see military action in Korea, where he had a distinguished war record, flying 66 combat missions in F-86 Sabre Jets and downing two mig-15s. He was subsequently an aerial gunnery instructor at Nellis Air Force Base in Nevada and increased his experience with jets as a F-100 Super Sabre flight commander in Bitburg Air Base in Germany from 1956-1959. A career in exploration followed seamlessly from his military record in the air. "It was a natural extension of being an aviation pilot and exploring the extremes of flight, when they were made available. I opened myself up to receive the benefits and to serve the best I could in the extension of those exploration boundaries."

Aldrin took a doctorate in astronautics from the Massachusetts Institute of Technology. His focus on manned space rendezvous was astute. It stood him in good stead as an aspiring astronaut and in 1963, at the age of 33, he joined NASA's elite band of pioneering astronauts. In 1966, as pilot on the *Gemini XII* orbital flight and rendezvous mission he established a new five-and-a-half-hour record for extended spacewalking. Three years after that success, he entered the annals of space exploration with the famous moonwalk. He was awarded the Presidential Medal for Freedom in the same year.

He became commander of the test pilot school at Edwards Air Force Base and resigned from NASA in 1971, having logged 289 hours and 53 minutes in space, including a shade under eight hours of extra-vehicular activity. A year later, he retired from the US Air Force after 21 years of service.

Some might have found the rest of life, after that unrepeatable moment reaching out into space with the hopes of humankind on his shoulders, immensely difficult on returning from the heavens to our everyday atmosphere. Aldrin's demons surfaced several years later. His battles against alcoholism and depression were chronicled in his 1973 autobiography *Return to Earth.*

However, Aldrin's success among the stars was followed by a stellar career on earth. He maintained his passion for space exploration with the founding of Starcraft Boosters Inc., a rocket design company. In 1998, he founded the ShareSpace Foundation, a non-profit organisation dedicated to making space tourism more affordable. He remains an ardent proponent of privatising space. Not content with entering the world of non-fiction, he penned two further science fiction novels, *Encounter with Tiber* (1996) and *The Return* (2000).

Aldrin gives short shrift to conspiracy theorists, who have long argued the moon landings were an elaborate hoax. In 2002, he was confronted by Bart Sibrel, one of his more obsessive stalkers, outside a Beverly Hills hotel. When Sibrel called him "a coward, a liar and a thief", the 72-year-old Aldrin reacted with aplomb and punched him in the face. Gratifyingly, the police did not press charges. In the same year, he was appointed by President Bush to the Presidential Commission on the Future of the United States Aerospace Industry.

Looking back on his career, Aldrin expresses the classic grit of the explorer faced with apparently insurmountable odds.

"No dream is too high for those with their eyes in the sky."

Aldrin, and his fellow astronauts, who were not allowed to keep any samples from their moonwalk, are still hoping they will be given a piece of moon rock one day. They have waited 36 years.

President Nixon laughing with astronauts.

Aboard the USS Hornet: *A happy President Richard Nixon laughs with* Apollo 11 *astronauts,*
left to right, Neil A. Armstrong, Michael Collins and Edwin E. Aldrin, Jr. as they exchange greetings
through the window of the Mobile Quarantine Facility aboard the USS Hornet, *1969.*

Sir WALLY HERBERT

It is a measure of Sir Wally Herbert's achievements as an explorer that he has a mountain range and plateau named after him in the Antarctic and another mountain named after him in the Arctic. Not many people alive today could boast something similar. That is certainly one measure of the man, but there are many others.

One could begin with the verdict of some of his contemporaries. Sir Ranulph Fiennes, for instance, who considers Herbert "the greatest explorer of our time". According to the late Lord Shackleton, he was simply a "phenomenon". In the words of Prince Charles, Herbert's "determination and courage are of such heroic proportions that his country should mark his achievements eventually by having him stuffed and put on display!"

Herbert has earned such accolades – and numerous awards – for one journey, above all others. It was widely regarded as the last great journey on earth and reached its climax on 6 April 1969, when Herbert, the expedition leader, reached the North Pole on foot. In the time-honoured way he sent a radio message to the Queen.

"I have the honour to inform your Majesty that today, 5th April, at 0700 hours Greenwich Meridian Time, the British Trans-Antarctic Expedition by dead reckoning reached the North Pole 407 days after setting out from Point Barrow, Alaska. My companions of the crossing party, Alan Gill, Major Kenneth Hedges, R.A.M.C., and Dr Roy Koerner, together with Squadron Leader Church, R.A.F., our radio relay officer at Point Barrow, are in good health and spirits and hopeful that by forced marches and a measure of good fortune the Expedition will reach Spitzbergen by

Midsummer's Day of this year, thus concluding in the name of our country the first surface crossing of the Arctic Ocean. (Signed W. Herbert, Expedition Leader)"

In fact, they had miscalculated, an error easily forgiven when one takes into account the formidable difficulties inherent in navigation at the North Pole in the pre-GPS era. They actually reached the pole a day later after a series of fresh marches and renewed calculations.

"Trying to set foot upon it had been like trying to step on the shadow of a bird that was hovering overhead,"

Herbert recalled in his book *Across the Top of the World*, "...for the surface across which we were moving was itself a moving surface on a planet that was spinning on its axis directly beneath our feet."

Whatever the final difficulties, it was a prodigious achievement. The British Prime Minister Harold Wilson described it "as a feat of endurance and courage which ranks with any in polar history". Over 464 days the expedition of three men and 40 dogs, carrying 32,000 kilograms of food and equipment, had traversed

3,800 route miles of frozen wilderness, recording the longest sustained polar journey in history and almost certainly the first surface crossing of the Arctic Ocean. The caveat stems from Peary's disputed claim to have reached the pole 60 years earlier, to the very day, a controversy that was reignited by Herbert in his 1989 biography, *Peary: The Noose of Laurels.*

Herbert was born in York in 1934 and grew up in South Africa. Trained at the School of Military Survey in Newbury, he subsequently joined the Royal Engineers in Egypt and on being demobbed after three years hitch-hiked back to England. He had no idea of how he might earn a living. Then, in 1955, something special happened.

"I was on a bus on my way to work one day (at the tender age of 20) when a newspaper fell into my lap from the overhead luggage rack. It was open at the 'Public Appointments' page, and my eye immediately caught an advertisement with the title: 'Expedition to Antarctica'. That was the first of a great many surprises and coincidences that have coloured my polar career."

Responding to the advertisement was a fateful step. It took Herbert to the 1955-1957 Falkland Island Dependencies Survey in Antarctica, where as surveyor he made the first map of the central plateau of the Antarctic Peninsula. Further expeditions followed, to Lapland, Svalbard and Greenland. In 1960, he joined the two-year New Zealand Antarctic expedition and with dog teams mapped on foot vast swathes of the Queen Maud range of mountains. To commemorate the 50th anniversary of Roald Amundsen's journey to the South Pole, Hebert retraced his return route down the Axel Heiberg Glacier, mapping the spectacular icefalls for the first time.

It was the Peary biography that unleashed a flood of venom from across the Atlantic, notably from the explorer's supporters "who had never seen pack ice let alone travelled on it", Herbert argues. They did not take kindly to the evidence he amassed indicating that the American could not have reached the North Pole as he had claimed. Opprobrium was heaped upon Herbert. The sneering continues to this day on websites attacking "sore British losers", and belittling "Wally's luxury marathon camping trip". In the words of one critic: "If Peary was 'The Man Who Refused to Fail' then Wally Herbert was 'the man Britain could not afford to let fail' after polar failures such as Franklin, Scott, Shackleton, Mawson, etc." Fuelled by nationalist pride, the controversy has refused to go away.

Physical challenges gave way to new interests after these epic polar journeys and it was Herbert's fascination with the Inuit which developed strongly from the early 1970s, when he lived with his wife Marie and daughter Kari in north-west Greenland for two years. Here and in the High Arctic travelling and hunting with the Eskimos he became keenly alive to the spiritual and mystical side of life. In his late sixties he discovered an artistic ability to which he gave free rein in pictures of sparkling polar landscapes and their fascinating wildlife.

Today, Herbert's position at the pinnacle of human exploration is assured. He has travelled 25,000 miles with dog teams, mapped 56,000 square miles of previously unexplored territory, and spent 15 years in the Antarctic and High Arctic. He takes a dim view of modern "glory seekers" and their "fearsome obsession to be either the first or the fastest". He sees himself as "the last of the fur-clad pioneers", an icon of the twentieth century.

'Crossing the North Pole' painted by Sir Wally Herbert.

"…With the original oil painting what I was looking for was a way of showing us 'crossing the North Pole' – not simply arriving at that point. The painting was inspired by the 16mm film we shot of our journey – by taking some clips from the sequence of crossing the North Pole and putting them together I gave the impression of 'crossing' the pole. The rays from the sun represent the longitudes at the North Pole through which we are passing, and the sun represents the pole itself. No one at that time had made a journey right across the Pole and this painting shows that achievement."

SVETLANA SAVITSKAYA

They say flying is in the blood, in which case the Russian cosmonaut Svetlana Savitskaya had a head start in life. Her father Yevgeniy Savitsky was the much-decorated World War II flying ace, deputy commander of the Soviet Air Defences and twice Hero of the Soviet Union.
In other words, a hard act to follow.

Born in Moscow in 1948, it took a while for Savitskaya to stare up at the skies for inspiration. Initially, at least, her parents encouraged more scholarly and traditional pursuits, keen to see her take up music, English and swimming. At school she was also a good sportswoman and took up running and figure skating.

If she could single out a moment in which flying and space exploration appeared to her as a possible destiny, it was on 6 August 1961, two days before her 13th birthday, when the Soviet cosmonaut Gherman Titov, launching on *Vostok 2*, became the second man in space. It was then she realised that Yuri Gagarin's tremendous feat was not a one-off, as she had originally thought. It was, instead, the harbinger of a new generation of space exploration, one in which she could play a part.

"It was something to be repeated, it was a new field of human activity that was going to last for a long time and something that I could do too and somehow I saw immediately that it was my path to be flying. I wanted to follow that road as a flight."

At 16, Savitskaya decided she would become a pilot, but was rejected as too young to start training. Instead, without her father's knowledge, she started parachuting. A year later, by which time her father had been let into her secret, she set a new record,

jumping from 14,252 metres, falling for 14 kilometres before opening her parachute at just 500 metres. Pilot training began in earnest at the age of 18 when she enrolled in the elite Moscow Aviation Institute.

In 1970, she wowed British spectators at the world acrobatics championship in Hullavington. She was dubbed 'Miss Sensation' by the British press after winning the world championship. It was, she acknowledges, a defining point in her career. "That victory meant so much for me because it gave me the moral right to say, 'Now I am the best and you cannot tell me I am not good enough for space travel or any more serious and sophisticated aircraft,' so that gave me the stimulus to seek a more advanced professional career. So after that I started flying jet planes and enrolled into the test-piloting school and each step was quite a hard one and I had to prove myself at each one."

Graduating from the Moscow Aviation Institute in 1972, it was not long before her obvious and prodigious talent propelled her into test-pilot school, where she soon started establishing new records in supersonic and turbo-prop aircraft, including the female record of 2,683 kilometres per hour in a mig-21. By 1980, she had succeeded in pushing herself forward into the team of cosmonauts. A Soviet women's team had been selected to undermine the American plan to send female astronauts up in the shuttle. In 1982 she became the second woman in space. Professionally, this was "the peak of my life. It was the realisation of everything I had dreamed of, of my goals in life that I had set for myself." Not content with that, she improved her space record on another mission two years later when, on 25 July 1984, she became the first woman to walk in space as part of the *Soyuz T-12* mission to conduct experiments on the *Salyut 7* space station.

It was a glorious moment, but Savitskaya, ever the professional, is not given to over-romanticising it. "For me professionalism is being able in any situation to just carry on with your work and I could describe all the beauties and emotions from outer space looking down onto the earth and I can do that, I know how to do that but I think that is the wrong approach," she argues. "For me it was mostly work, it was a very hard and serious programme that I had to carry out and in order to be able to do that you have to be professional and have not just your training but very good psychological training. Those cosmonauts that describe all the things that they experienced in space, 'I saw earth floating beneath me' and all those beautiful words, I think it is not professional."

Her best-known mission in space was also her last. In 1987 she became deputy to the chief designer of Energia and two years later entered politics as a member of the Russian parliament. She retired as a cosmonaut in 1993.

For Savitskaya's generation, growing up as children with the Sputnik launches in the late 1950s, space exploration was an exciting new frontier. Awareness of the benefits of space exploration was widespread in the Soviet Union at that time, she remembers. Nowadays, however, she believes the initial excitement has cooled down. As missions into space have become more routine, paradoxically there appears to be less understanding of why we continue to press forward in and across space.

"Now when I give lectures to students in various colleges and universities and I ask the question, 'Why would humanity want this, why would we need to go to space?' they do not have a clear idea. I have to explain it to them, whereas in our times, you could ask anyone and people could explain the benefits to you. Now it is something more routine and not so much interest as there used to be in my time."

Savitskaya recalls a slightly neglected Russian saying to inspire the next generation of explorers: "We cannot wait for nature to show mercy on us. To achieve what we can ourselves is our goal."

For this fiercely determined woman, there is no great mystery about how to succeed in life, as an explorer or otherwise. It always comes down to those two old favourites.

"Patience and hard work will get you everything in life."

Svetlana Savitskaya wearing a space suit.

19 August 1982

REINHOLD MESSNER

In Shakespeare's **Julius Caesar,** *Cassius marvels at Caesar's protean powers, how*

" ...he doth bestride the narrow world

Like a Colossus... "

When one surveys the history of twentieth-century mountain-eering, one man bestrides the scene with equal dominance: Messner. His surname alone evokes pioneering epics of survival at the highest altitude, images of a smiling man whose face, almost entirely hidden by hair, is more 1970s, rock star than mountaineering legend. First to climb Everest without oxygen in 1978 with Peter Habeler, he went on to become the first man to climb all 14 of the world's 8,000-metre peaks. And, as is inevitable with such extraordinary success, there have always been critics who have made all sorts of sniping comments, from accusing him of having brain damage after prolonged exposure to extreme altitude, to leaving other mountaineers to die on mountains in his overriding bid to reach the top, come what may. Yet the criticisms fail to remove him from his legitimate throne at the very pinnacle of mountaineering greatness. There is no one quite like him. And now, because he has achieved what he has, there never can be.

Messner was born among the mountains in 1944 in Villnöss in the South Tyrol. Climbing, therefore, was always an entirely natural pursuit. "For me it was quite logical. I was brought up in the Dolomites – the most beautiful rock areas of the world – and we had no swimming pool, no football pitch, so there wasn't the opportunity to do much else and so we went off and we climbed these rocks. The children in the valley did not do this as they

had other activities to follow, the cows and doing things in the fields with other small children. We being one daughter and eight sons of a teacher, we went climbing and a few of us became extreme climbers and when I was five I did my first 3,000-metre climb with the parents and mostly later ascents with my brother and when I was 20 I did my first ascent on the Dolomites and all over the Alps."

By his early twenties, Messner was well down the path that would mark him out as a true original in his field. In an era of 'siege' mountaineering in which climbers on the tallest peaks ferried equipment up and down to fixed camps to prepare their way to the top on fixed ropes, Messner forged his own very different route. His approach was far simpler and purer, in a sense less an-tagonistic to the mountain. It involved translating the alpine style to the Himalayas and other great ranges, in short lightweight expeditions and lightning ascents. He called it 'Renunciation Alpinism', a rejection of oxygen apparatus, fixed high camps, high-altitude porters. It was self-sufficiency.

His first eight-thousander, Nanga Parbat, came in 1970, but brought tragedy with it in the death of his climbing partner and younger brother Gunther, killed in an avalanche. The others followed steadily over the next two decades, their names familiar to anyone with an interest in this higher world: Manaslu,

Hidden Peak, the landmark Everest climb, where he described himself summiting as "nothing more than a single gasping lung", followed by the supremely difficult K2, and Shisha Pangma. A 'hat-trick' of eight-thousanders in 1982 (itself a first for a single season) – Kangchenjunga, Gasherbrum II and Broad Peak – gave birth to his dream of climbing all 14, though he rejects the idea he was ever 'collecting' them. There followed Cho Oyu, Annapurna, Dhaulagiri and Makalu. In 1986, 16 years after his first ascent of Nanga Parbat, he descended safely from Lhotse and the record was his, whether he liked it or not.

"Luckily, climbing is not capable of being expressed either in terms of records or by numbers," he wrote in *All 14 Eight-Thousanders*. "It certainly cannot be measured in seconds, metres of height or grades."

"I was lucky, the Gods were kind to me… We all need luck, for the mountains are infinitely bigger than us. Mere men can never 'vanquish' them. 'Lhagyelo', the Tibetans say whenever they venture up a mountain or a high pass, and I say it too: 'The Gods have won'."

Much of that is true, of course, but mountaineering can be sufficiently recorded and measured to enable us to acknowledge Messner as its greatest ever practitioner. He does not consider himself an explorer. His challenge has always been personal, a question of survival rather than science. "I would like to use the word adventure for my activities but not exploration," he states. "Adventuring for me is nothing but the path for surviving. I have exposed myself to high places, cold places, windy places, to dangerous places generally and I try to survive. The whole energy I put in is only to survive in these difficult places and the more dangerous and difficult they are the more difficult it is to

survive. So the best adventurer is a woman or a man who is accepting all risks and is surviving. The person who is dying in the first or second expedition is not a good adventurer."

The personal challenges have continued beyond the mountains. In 1990, he made the first crossing of Antarctica on foot, via the South Pole, covering 1,750 miles in 92 days. In 1995, he stated publicly that he had stopped high-altitude climbing, turning his attentions to the Arctic, which he attempted to cross from Siberia to Canada. He has written more than 40 books about his adventures, including his quest for the yeti, which he said he discovered in the form of a Tibetan bear. He went into politics in 1999, serving one term as a member of the European Parliament for the Italian Green Party.

"I am an explorer of my own fear, of my own hopes, of my own dreams, my own possibilities, and in reality my activity is nothing but a passion for limits."

He has helped define them on the summits of the world.

"As far as the public is concerned, since 1978 my sensational climbs –
Everest without oxygen and Nanga Parbat solo – are unsurpassable."

Nanga Parbat, 2000

Sir RICHARD BRANSON

When a British businessman has been a regular fixture in the upper echelons of the **Sunday Times** *Rich*

List for years, has been feted by both Conservative and Labour parties alike, and has received a

knighthood for his services to commerce, you could be forgiven for thinking he was more likely to be

Mr Pinstripe Establishment than Maverick Pirate Rogue.

But Sir Richard Branson has long delighted in confounding expectations. And in later years, the flamboyant, tousle-haired, goatee-bearded knight has been earning his spurs as something of an explorer.

Business came first. Born in 1950, Branson enjoyed a private education, first at prep school, later at Stowe, the Buckinghamshire school for well-heeled boys and girls. Here he displayed his entrepreneurial talents early on by setting up a successful student advisory service and newspaper, *Student*. The headmaster's now famous reaction was surprisingly prescient as Branson left in 1967. "Congratulations, Branson," he said. "I predict that you will either go to prison or become a millionaire." In the event, he did both.

School was not a success academically. Branson was too busy running the magazine to worry about grades and when exams came, he wasn't averse to cheating. In any case, he was a dyslexic before the condition was properly understood. "Since nobody had ever heard of dyslexia, being unable to read, write, or spell just meant to the rest of the class and the teachers that you were either stupid or lazy." He was neither but the experience taught him to concentrate and made him more intuitive, he says.

With school behind him, he was able to pour all his energies into business. At the ripe age of 20, he set up Virgin as a mail-order record retailer, followed quickly by a music shop in the heart of Oxford Street. Virgin's first signed artist went on to bankroll Branson for several years. It was Mike Oldfield, whose album *Tubular Bells*, anthem of the 1970s, sold more than 5 million copies, one of Britain's bestselling albums ever. More coups followed, notably the signing in 1977 of The Sex Pistols, who were at the time *personae non gratae* at every other record label in the country. Virgin's tally of artists signed over the years is a roll call of rock and roll and pop, from Steve Winwood, Genesis and Phil Collins to Peter Gabriel, Simple Minds, Bryan Ferry and the Rolling Stones. Names such as these helped Branson sell the Virgin Music Group – albeit reluctantly and with well-publicised tears – to Thorn EMI for an eye-watering $1 billion in 1992.

Today, the Virgin brand seems worryingly ubiquitous, from trains and planes to mobile phones, pet insurance and wines. As Peter Gabriel once commented: "It's outrageous! Virgin is becoming everything. You wake up in the morning to Virgin Radio; you put on your Virgin Jeans; you go to the Virgin Megastore; you drink Virgin Cola; you fly to America on Virgin Atlantic. Soon you'll be offering Virgin births, Virgin marriages and Virgin funerals." From the mid-1980s, Branson decided to take Virgin into new, record-breaking realms of adventure, over water and across the skies. The ventures were born both of his thrill for excitement as a pioneer of speed and an unrivalled opportunity for brand publicity.

In 1986, his boat *Virgin Atlantic Challenger II* smashed the record for the fastest crossing of the Atlantic. The following year, he began what has since become a compelling love affair with ballooning. He put down a marker with *Virgin Atlantic Flyer*, the first hot-air balloon to cross the Atlantic. It set a record, too, for sheer size with a capacity of 2.3 million cubic feet. In 1991, he went a step further, crossing the Pacific Ocean from Japan to Arctic Canada, a distance of 6,700 miles, establishing another record in the process. The balloon had grown to 2.6 million cubic feet, the speed from 130mph to up to 245mph.

> **"One of the most magical things about ballooning is that the wind is inaudible because the balloon is travelling at the same speed as the wind."**

"Flying at 150 miles an hour, one can put a tissue paper on the capsule which, in theory, shouldn't blow off. And so although we were in the middle of a snowstorm, it was very quiet," he said of his adopted sport.

Though frequently pilloried as a publicity-hungry mogul, Branson argues that his high-profile ballooning can play an important role in advancing scientific knowledge. "Quite often from personal challenges, science is pushed forward," he told one interviewer. "For instance, the ozone layer, which is being damaged by all the pollution that's being pumped into it. It's very difficult to know just how badly damaged it is and in what particular place in the world it's the most damaged. If we're

successful in flying around the world in a manned balloon, and if we craft the technology for other manned ballooned attempts to take place in the future, then the ozone-testing equipment that we're taking on in this trip could become commonplace in other manned balloons in future years. And by really carefully monitoring how badly the ozone is being damaged, that can alert countries and governments to act much quicker than they, perhaps, have acted up to now. I think that could be one of the most important things that comes from this trip as far as future science is concerned."

That round-the-world bid was unsuccessful and in the end Branson was pipped to the post by Bertrand Piccard and Brian Jones in 1999. Some consolation came with the publication that year of his typically brash autobiography *Losing My Virginity: How I've Survived, Had Fun, And Made a Fortune Doing Business My Way.*

But defeat does not come easily – or naturally – to a man like Branson. It was only to be expected, then, that he should turn his sights on another record, this time a non-stop flight around the world. Cue balloonist Steve Fossett and the *GlobalFlyer*, with Branson as lead sponsor. On 3 March 2005, Fossett touched down safely into the record books after a flight lasting 67 hours 1 minute, averaging almost 300mph.

Space is Branson's latest frontier. In 2004, he signed a £14 million contract for five 'spaceliners' for his new company Virgin Galactic, which aims to sell tickets for a first round of space travel in 2008. The price for a taste of space? A cool $200,000.

Around the world in a balloon in less than 18 days.

Marrakech, Morocco, 7 January 1997

BRADFORD and BARBARA WASHBURN

You could say Bradford Washburn was an early starter when it came to mountaineering, photography and writing. But that would hardly do justice to the man. Born in Cambridge, Massachusetts in 1910, by 1926 he had climbed Mont Blanc, the Matterhorn and Monte Rosa and had written his first book, a guide to the White Mountains of the eastern United States (his second book came at 17).

Armed with a Kodak Brownie, his 13th birthday present, he was also well on his way to making his mark as a photographer, if not quite a mapmaker and surveyor *sans pareil*. Thee years later, at the seasoned age of 19, he was elected to the French Alpine Club's prestigious Groupe de Haute Montagne. He has never been one for time-wasting.

In 1933 he graduated from Harvard University and stayed on as an instructor at its Institute of Geographical Exploration from 1935-1942. At a still precocious 29 he was appointed director of the Boston Society of Natural History – later renamed the Museum of Science – which over the next 41 years he built up from a crusty institution into a world-renowned, dynamic centre of science. All this while he carved out a sterling mountaineering career, married to his other great loves, Barbara, their three children and photography.

He has made eight first-recorded ascents of North American peaks and has compiled around two dozen maps, notably those of Mount Everest, Mount McKinley and the Grand Canyon which remain, years later, state of the art. His black-and-white landscape photography, typically high-resolution and large-format, wonderfully evokes the bold grandeur of the mountain world, all stately glaciers, chiselled ridges and pristine peaks. His 1937 collection of aerial photographs of the White Mountains are stark portraits, breathtaking to behold. How many shivering hours has he spent precariously hanging out of aeroplanes to record these images? One shudders to imagine.

Obsessive, gruff and feisty are words often used to describe Bradford. Without such qualities, he probably would not have achieved half as much during his long, ground-breaking, mountain-shooting career. Asked what exploration means to him, he fires back: "It means I have a damn good wife," before adding,

"The best part of exploration is the people that you do it with."

A reference not only to expedition colleagues but his beloved Barbara, with whom he shares his most cherished award, the Centennial Award of the National Geographic Society.

Barbara is a little more forthcoming. "Exploration is sharing the thrill of entering into a new area that nobody has been to or mapped."

She says, "Brad had done that before I even met him. To name two, Mounts King George and Queen Mary – he was there in

Jubilee year in 1937. That is real exploration. They mapped out the whole area. We got a great personal letter from King George V for that one."

Had she not listened to a friendly postman, Barbara would never have met the man she has been married to for more than 60 years. One day he suggested she go for an interview with the by now famous Bradford, who was looking to recruit an assistant. Barbara's initial response was not promising. She told him she didn't want to work "in that stuffy old museum", nor did she want to have anything to do with "a crazy mountain climber". But she went ahead with it against her better judgement.

"My aim was to get the interview over as soon as possible," she reminisces. "So I had my interview with Brad, I had never laid eyes on him but he was a very famous explorer and he was fairly nice but he said I had to handle all the finances of this museum, which I had no idea about. He quite forcefully told me that I could learn, couldn't I? When I left he said he would give me two weeks to think about it. He ended up calling me every night. I kept thinking that if this guy is going to be so persistent and aggressive that this museum is going to go places and that will make for an interesting job." She took it. They were engaged within the year, mutually smitten, and married in 1940.

Apart from raising three children, the Washburns have pursued careers both separate – he as a museum man, she as a remedial teacher – and together, particularly among the mountains, which has drawn both to write books about their extraordinary experiences. The very title of Barbara's recent memoir *The Accidental Adventurer* encapsulates her modesty while *Exploring the Unknown* tells the gripping tale of Bradford's numerous expeditions in Alaska and the Yukon.

Together they established what has become the most popular route up McKinley, a mountain that gave Barbara one of her most remarkable moments in 1947 when she became the first woman to reach the summit. "When I got to the top I thought, well here I am, and I will never be here again and I was freezing, it was very cold, we were there for an hour at 22 below zero. I thought I had better go and look at the view. So I walked over to the edge and I thought this is just how I remembered heaven when I was a little girl, big white billowy clouds with blue sky in between. I knew that, even though I didn't give a rip about being the first woman on top, that somebody was going to say I was the first woman on top and make a fuss."

At 95, Bradford is less optimistic about the future of the planet than he once was. "I think the biggest problem that we've got in the world today is overpopulation," he growls. "Nobody has got the guts to face up to it. I think that the people on it will eventually destroy our world. They're going to destroy nature, at least. Men are going to destroy each other, because people don't want to realise what really is going on. It's so dreadful that they don't care. They want to say, 'Let's keep on going and hope it won't happen.'"

The photographic treasures he has left us of an untrammelled mountain world remind us of how it once was.

"A compulsive problem solver, Washburn would remove the door of an airplane and muscle his 50-pound camera into position using a spiderweb of ropes, lashing himself in to keep from being sucked into the void."

Bradford Washburn and the Fairchild K-6 camera and
the Fairchild 71 monoplane, Valdez, Alaska, 1937.

ROBERT SWAN OBE

Ever since Scott and Shackleton, the British have had an enduring fascination and love affair with the North and South Poles. Robert Swan is no different, only he took his passion out of the armchair and onto the ice, becoming the first person to walk to both ends of the earth. Shaven-headed, with eyes that bore into you with sheer intensity, he has the driven look of a Russian cosmonaut from the 1960s.

Inspiration came early. He was born in County Durham in 1956 and as an 11-year-old was captivated by the film *Scott of the Antarctic*, starring Sir John Mills. "It fascinated me that there was this place off the map and that nobody owned it. I was very much drawn to the history of Antarctica, the people and what they were all about. I asked myself how I would fit into a scenario such as that," he says. "It really began because I was inspired to love history at school by a great teacher who made history the most exciting part of my education."

There was another moment of discovery while Swan was studying at Durham University. Same film, ten years later.

"I hired an entire cinema for a private viewing of **Scott of the Antarctic.** *I wanted it to be a formal moment, so put on a dinner jacket and a bow tie. I got up at the end of it and said, right, I'm going to do it, I'm going to walk to the South Pole. I don't care how long it takes, I'm doing it."*

The determination led him directly to the planning stage of the expedition he named 'In the Footsteps of Scott'. From 1979-1984, he was immersed in research and fundraising, generating more than £2.5 million from 200 sponsors. This expedition was undertaken in a truly traditional way, which meant the team reached Antarctica by ship and then lived together for nine months during the winter, before the journey started.

On 11 January 1986, after 883 miles on foot without radio communications, Swan and his companions Roger Mear and Gareth Wood reached the South Pole. The Queen honoured their achievement at completing the longest unsupported march in history with the presentation of the Polar Medal.

No sooner had Swan achieved this early childhood goal than he set about complementing it with a journey to the North Pole. This time he managed to raise £3.7 million from 500 sponsors for 'Icewalk', an unusual expedition which combined an eight-man assault on the Pole together with the world's first international student expedition into the Arctic. He reached his goal on 14 May 1989, becoming the first person to walk to both poles.

Swan sees this achievement as a beginning rather than the end of the journey. He is a thoughtful commentator on modern exploration and remains unimpressed by headline-grabbing stunts which are full of sound and fury and signify nothing. Perhaps it is the historian in him. "The world is full of people who want to be something, to be the first to do this or that, and there is nothing at all wrong in that," he acknowledges. "But unless that desire evolves into something more significant, the whole exercise becomes pointless. I think part of one's drive is originally or initially to do something to say, hi, here I am. You then realise that actually that means nothing at all, absolutely nothing. All the effort that you make only means something if you then evolve it into something that makes true sense. It's a madness, a paradox where you have to do something completely ridiculous, perhaps, even stupid, as well as egotistical, in order to actually end up trying to do something that means something."

Swan should know what he's talking about. In his case, his experiences at the poles demonstrated the dangers of environmental damage at the icecaps. On his South Pole journey, the hole in the ozone layer badly affected his eyes and he suffered long-lasting skin damage to his face. Then at the North Pole, he and his companions were almost drowned because of the melting ice caused by global warming. Personal experience has since evolved into a public mission to persuade policy-makers of the urgent need to address environmental challenges.

In 1989, the same year he completed his landmark expedition to the North Pole, he was appointed United Nations Goodwill Ambassador for youth. His passion for raising awareness of environmental issues took him to the Earth Summit in Rio de Janeiro in 1992, where he was a keynote speaker. Two years later, he was appointed Special Envoy to the Director-General of UNESCO and in 1995 was awarded an OBE.

Swan then committed himself to inspire youth on the issue of survival on earth by taking large groups of students and young explorers to Antarctica. In 2002, after five years of battling, he removed 1,000 tons of rubbish from Bellingshausen, the Russian

Antarctic Station, and set up the first Antarctic Education Station as a global resource for teachers.

The next adventure sees Swan and his team on a circumnavigation of the Americas via the North West Passage, embarking from San Francisco in 2007, a century after Amundsen's groundbreaking journey. This time, the focus is on the need to look for alternative sources of energy. It could hardly happen at a more timely moment.

"We need to be looking at using more renewable energy on earth. We cannot simply just keep going on using more and more oil. So we're sailing our *Yacht 2041*, complete with sails made from recyclable materials and an engine that runs on bio-diesel. People need to recognise that the use of fossil fuels must come to an end. We've got to look seriously at commercially using renewable energy."

Swan's example has already provided motivation for many young explorers and students. To inspire others he quotes Goethe: "Whatever you can do or dream you can, begin it. Boldness has genius, power and magic in it."

"The last great exploration left on earth is to survive on it."

"Great feats are rarely achieved by individuals in isolation; more often it is team effort.
A team which understands its strengths and weaknesses and pulls together to face the
challenge will achieve the seemingly impossible."

Robert Swan OBE

Photo: Robert and his mother Margaret Swan in Hyde Park, May 1989,
hours after his return from the North Pole.

JOHN BLASHFORD-SNELL OBE

Colonel John Blashford-Snell is as imposing and impressive as his name (with a rich, military voice to match). Just as it seems to carry faint echoes of nineteenth-century exploration, so Blashford-Snell, a silver-haired tower of a man, looks as though he has just stepped out of a nineteenth-century jungle, all safari suit and room-filling bonhomie.

At 70, his robust physique suggests that were he to give you a hearty slap on the back, which is always a possibility, he would probably send you flying.

Born in 1936, Blashford-Snell was educated at Victoria College, Jersey. His father was an army chaplain and left the island with Blashford-Snell's mother to work as missionaries in New Zealand. The explorer credits his parents, who were forever rushing around the South Island on horses organising excursions with Boy Scouts and Girl Guides in the 1920s, with instilling a desire to get out and explore his environment.

Following his father's example, he joined the army, where he saw active service with the Royal Engineers in a career lasting 37 years.

"I wanted to be a sapper as they are known to be the explorers of the army, and they positively encouraged me because they make maps and find ways of getting railways or roads over mountains, through forests and across swamps. They are the army's obstacle breakers in peace and war."

Blashford-Snell's interest in exploration and expeditions was formalised with his posting to the Royal Military Academy at Sandhurst as an instructor in the mid-1960s. Little knowing what lay in wait for him, he was collared by General Sir John Mogg, the tremendously popular Canadian-born commandant who told him he was going to be the adventure training officer. "Your job is quite simple," the general said. "Get as many of these little blighters overseas for the benefit of their character and the least possible detriment to the empire." For a man of boundless energy and insatiable wanderlust, what could be a more stimulating job? Blashford-Snell, or Blashers, as he is widely known, rose magnificently to the challenge.

A natural leader of the British Army expedition which made the first descent of the Blue Nile in 1968 at the invitation of Emperor Haile Selassie of Ethiopia, he followed this landmark success a year later by founding the Scientific Exploration Society to "foster and encourage scientific exploration" worldwide. In 1971-1972, he led the first vehicle crossing of the entire Darien Gap and the expedition to navigate the Zaire River in 1974-1975. Between 1978-1992, he set up and led Operations Drake and Raleigh with the assistance of the Prince of Wales, overseeing 10,000 young men and women from 50 countries fanning out across the world on worthwhile projects and expeditions. Had his legacy as an explorer consisted simply of Drake and Raleigh, household names for anyone who grew up in the late 1970s and

1980s, Blashford-Snell's legacy would already be assured. It is typical of the man and his good-humoured, boundless energy that he should have embarked on a series of fresh challenges, still organised by the Scientific Exploration Society, as well as numerous charitable works in the UK, mainly for the benefit of disadvantaged youth.

For Blashford-Snell, the purpose inherent in his expeditions has always been fundamental. A military man through and through, he is not interested in gimmicks, stunts or a physical challenge, no matter how tough, just for the sake of it. He says,

"I define an adventurer as someone who goes to the ends of the earth to find out something about themselves. An explorer is one that travels to learn out about flora and fauna and the place and the people to bring back knowledge."

"So when people ask me whether I am an adventurer I say 'I hope not'. That's really my way of looking at exploration. If someone asked me to climb Everest I'd probably put a scaffolding up the side. I am not interested in a personal challenge. I'm not saying there is anything wrong with people who are but the actually physical purpose doesn't grip me."

In 1992, he retired from the army but the expeditions continued. It was almost as though they could never stop. "Curiosity is my biggest driving force, it's my interest in people and flora and fauna that really drives me on," he says. "I love a challenge and if someone says to me it can't be done or we don't know how this can be done my ears always prick up."

Such was his reaction when he was asked by the priest of the Wai-Wai tribe in Guyana if he could bring them a grand piano. Blashford-Snell immediately recognised it as a good story, but more importantly an opportunity to raise enough money to save the tribe which was the natural guardian of a unique area of pristine forest. "If that tribe leaves that area which is about the size of Wales, the loggers and illegal miners will flood in and it will be decimated," he argues. That proposition was simple enough, but procuring and transporting a grand piano across such difficult terrain was enough to give most people a headache.

"I said 'Good God, have you any idea what a grand piano looks like?' and the priest said 'I've seen pictures of one'. I didn't think he'd ever be able to play it and I remarked on that and he said 'No, no, we are musical people', adding 'God moves in mysterious ways'."

It goes without saying that the mission in 2000 to deliver the 800lb grand piano across steamy jungle, swamp, river and mountain was a success. The tribe took to piano playing with a speed and skill that caught the explorer and his team by surprise. Only a man like John Blashford-Snell would have had the thoughtfulness and style to send a piano-tuning expedition back two years later.

"Curiosity is my biggest driving force, it's my interest in people and flora and fauna that really drives me on."

Colonel John Blashford-Snell

Giant elephant quest, Nepal, 1997

ANDREW MITCHELL

Let us be grateful, first that the rainforest canopy explorer Andrew Mitchell got a fateful crick in his neck in Borneo in 1978 and second, that he has got a decent head for heights.

To deal with his neck first: "I originally became interested in the canopy whilst surveying primates in Borneo," he explains. "I constantly got a crick in my neck from staring upwards at small black silhouettes jumping around the branches and became intrigued as to what their high-rise world was like. Surrounded in the emerald gloom of the understorey, it became clear to me that most studies of tropical forests had been conducted in the equivalent of the underground car park, while all the interesting things were going on up in the penthouse."

In other words, the scientific community had to raise its sights. Mitchell was well placed to lead the way. Born in Jersey in 1953 and inspired by Gerald Durrell, he studied zoology at Bristol University before moving to the Scientific Exploration Society, where from 1977-1982 he was its scientific co-ordinator with responsibility for the research activities of its field projects worldwide. He got a taste for combining exploration, science and adventure while directing biological, archaeological and medical research programmes on two of the world's largest international expeditions, Operations Drake and Raleigh. It was on these that he pioneered the use of light, aerial walkways in the tropical rainforest canopy that would allow the world's first comparative study of this extraordinary and unknown world where almost half of all life on earth exists.

Onto his head for heights; he says:

"Make no mistake, going up into the canopy is dangerous. It's three million years ago since we were up there and we're not very good at leaping among branches any more! Fifty to sixty metres up, it can be quite frightening. If you fall, you die."

Frightening it undoubtedly must be, but insufficiently scary to deter Mitchell from a subsequent career amid the teetering treetops. The hitherto virtually unexplored environment, one of the last great biological frontiers, was simply too exciting to ignore. Today, Mitchell and his scientific colleagues use towers, balloons, and even giant construction cranes helicoptered into the forest to access the canopy. "These are our ships on which we explore an unknown green ocean," he says.

Mitchell was appointed the Rufford Research Fellow in Environmental Understanding at Green College, Oxford, in 2002. Something of a rarity for an academic, he is also an experienced broadcaster, an excellent communicator with an enviable way of transmitting the sense of discovery that is at the heart of his work. "It is a realm of flying frogs, and gliding snakes," he enthuses. "Trees conduct their sex lives in the canopy, luring bees, birds and bats into complex relationships with their flowers in order to pass their genes around.

Numerous creatures spend their whole lives there without ever coming down to the ground, and plants, too, have colonised the tree crowns as botanical hitchhikers. The canopy is where life meets the atmosphere. It fills our lungs with oxygen, breaths rain across the globe and sifts pollutants from the air. It is a complex guardian tending the health of the planet, as delicate and important to the earth as the lining of our lungs is to us."

In fact, the canopy is thought to contain around 40 per cent of the world's terrestrial biodiversity. A single tree in Amazonian Peru may contain more than 40 species of ants, on a par with the entire number throughout the UK. The words 'thought' and 'may' are instructive. We don't know precisely. Exploration here is a work in progress. It has been said that we know more about the surface of the moon than we do about the tops of the trees.

"We're dealing with the richest, least known, most threatened habitat on earth," Mitchell continues. "The problem with our understanding of forests is that nearly all the information we have has been gleaned from just two metres above the soil, and yet we're dealing with tropical trees that grow to heights of 80 metres or, in the case of the tallest redwood, 112 metres. It's like doctors trying to treat humans by only looking at their feet."

He co-founded the Earthwatch Institute in the UK and, after working as the Vice President of Program Development and International Relations at its headquarters in Boston, returned to Oxford in 2000. He decided to follow his instincts for discovery and with the support of the Rufford Foundation in the UK launched the Global Canopy Foundation in 2001. Over the next five years he established the Global Canopy Programme, of which he is the Executive Director.

Judging by the programme's progress since then, Mitchell has been as active and successful out of the trees as he has among them. In 2003, he convened the 'Canopy Summit' in the Royal Botanic Gardens in Kew, launching a worldwide campaign to set up a network of 20 'Whole Forest Observatories' around the world in biodiversity hot spots such as Latin America, Africa, India and Asia. The aim is to investigate the interface between life and the atmosphere and the potential impact of climate change on forest canopies.

His campaign has already started to pay off. In 2005, the UN Environment Programme and the Global Environment Facility agreed to back the project supporting the first five observatories – in Brazil, Ghana, Madagascar, India and Malaysia. "I was inspired by our eighteenth century astronomical observatory at Green College, in Oxford," he says.

A driven man, Mitchell has been no slouch when it comes to literary output. He is the author of seven books, including the highly acclaimed study *The Enchanted Canopy: Secrets from the Rainforest Roof.*

Like a number of other explorers in this book, he remains passionately committed to the preservation of the fragile rainforest. "History will judge that all our efforts in rainforest conservation over the last 30 years add up to little more than the charge of the 'lite' brigade. Conservation needs to out-compete commercialism," he insists. "Currently, it cannot. It is a question of how we value things. The canopy offers a new perspective, a new set of values connecting life, atmosphere and people."

"Sixty metres up in a giant rainforest tree in the heart of Borneo gives you a different view of life. Only the sea bed and the soil can rival the rainforest canopy as nature's most unexplored realm. Here, half of all life on earth meets the atmosphere and is on a collision course with climate change. The consequences for humankind are unknown, something Andrew Mitchell and the teams of scientists he leads in the Global Canopy Programme are intent on finding out."

Andrew Mitchell

Borneo

BORGE OUSLAND

Those explorers who seek the ultimate test of their abilities against the extremes of nature know better than most that there is no success without risking failure. Colonel Norman Vaughan, the veteran polar explorers motto: "Dream big and dare to fail." The Norwegian polar explorer Borge Ousland thinks along the same lines.

"If you want to be better, you have to give yourself another chance, take the chance of making another failure," he says. "In order to win, you have to risk losing. That's part of it."

Ousland knows all about risk-taking, and confronting failure. He has done both. In fact, his expeditions revel in risk. Two words tend to feature in any Ousland expedition: solo and unsupported.

The first of his expeditions in this line came in 1991, a solo trek to the North Pole, hard on the heels of a joint unsupported ski trek to the same place, which itself was a first. It made the exploration community sit up and listen to the Norwegian, who was soon receiving considerable publicity. "I've started to feel the layers of civilization peeling away; it takes weeks to find your animal self," he wrote in *National Geographic* during that pioneering expedition. "I wake up, grunt at the sun, perform the day's chores, sniff the north wind, and automatically pick out the best route and the safest campsites – all without thought. I've found the rhythm. I think I can do this." Fifty-two gruelling days after setting off from Cape Arktichesky, he did. He still considers it his greatest moment out in the field. "Not many believed I would make it, I was not really sure myself."

Born in Oslo in 1962, Ousland went on to train as a diver after leaving school and for a decade from the mid-1980s worked in the North Sea as a saturation diver. In 1986, he dipped his toes into the exploration world, skiing across Greenland with friends, travelling 500 miles in 37 days in an expedition which recalled the exploits of his fellow countryman Fritjof Nansen a century earlier.

Though he finds it hard to define exactly, Ousland is in no doubt about why he has chosen the path of adventure and exploration. "I think there is this restlessness in me, this urge to do it. I cannot explain why. There is a lot of enthusiasm, I really feel great when I do these expeditions and I love it. I think you have to really love it to do these hard trips. You can't do hard trips for money or for glory or any of those kinds of reasons. It's really the true and joyful memories of being out there and being so close to you and close to nature. That's why I do it."

He regards exploration as an intensely individual experience.

"Exploration is very personal. It doesn't have to be the North Pole or the South Pole. I think the most important aspect of exploration is that you start on a personal level, you have to start at some level you are comfortable with and work from there. For me it is seeking out what is beyond the next horizon, it's about following your dreams. I don't do it for exercise, I do not do it to set a rulebook but for adventure."

From 1989 until 1991, Ousland donned uniform, serving out his military service with the Norwegian Special Naval Forces. He followed the trailblazing solo unsupported trek to the North Pole with its mirror image – only longer – at the other end of the world, an attempt to trek solo and unsupported across Antarctica from coast to coast via the South Pole in 1995. That time he had to abort but, unable to countenance defeat, he crossed the continent again in 1996-1997, travelling 1,778 miles in 64 days, enduring temperatures as low as minus 56 degrees Celsius. In 2001, Ousland became the first to cross the Arctic solo – inevitably – from Siberia to Canada via the North Pole. That epic journey took him 82 days. Ousland's relentless preference for solo travel is borne out in the titles of his books, *Alone to the North Pole* (1994), *Alone Across Antarctica* (1997) and *Alone Across the North Pole* (2001).

Wherever he goes, one of his most important must-haves is a collection of 50 or 60 poems. "I pick one every day and read it and I can go and think about that poem. There is a Norwegian poet I really like who writes lots about the woods and nature of Norway and that's something I really long for anywhere I go. Especially out there on the ice where there is no grass or trees, there is nothing, it is a very desolate place so I long for the woods where every square centimetre is full of life and trees and birds and everything."

From the poles, Ousland turned to dabble in mountains, climbing Cho Oyu in 1999 and reaching the south summit of Everest in 2003 before returning to the ice by making the first unsupported trek across the Patagonian Ice Field, the third largest glacier in the world, in the same year.

He understands he is an inspirational figure for untold numbers of young adventurers and throws himself into his role as a motivational speaker with the same sort of intensity that characterises his extreme expeditions. His message to them is straightforward and uncompromising.

"I do have a motto and that is, follow your dream, never stop. I think it is our own responsibility to make young people understand and respect nature because only by using nature we will learn to take care of it. I think everyone needs an anchor and that's the most important thing we can give our kids. So in that respect I hope I can be an inspiration to others through my expeditions, pictures and other work."

"Follow your dream, never stop! People can build their willpower deliberately. We are born with a certain amount, but that is just a platform. I think you can build willpower and be strong and achieve a lot."

Borge Ousland

March 1994, on his solo and unsupported trip to the North Pole.

ROBERT BALLARD

In his own mind, Robert Ballard's greatest achievement is the discovery of hydrothermal vents off the Galapagos Islands. To everyone else, he is the man who found the Titanic*.*

As a child, when not swimming, scuba diving, surfing or studying tidal pools around his home city of San Diego, he was immersed in adventure books like Jules Verne's *Twenty Thousand Leagues Under the Sea*, a combination of interests which drew him inexorably towards marine geology. "I fell in love with the sea and the hidden land beneath its surface," he says when asked how he got started in exploration. "I think growing up at the water's edge in an environment like southern California, which is on the frontier of a pioneering country and a family history of moving west," only added to his underwater wanderlust.

With his nose stuck in Jules Verne, Ballard's childhood hero was the inimitable Captain Nemo. "I wanted to be an undersea explorer," he recalls. "Fortunately, when I told my parents, they didn't laugh at me. They actually encouraged me to live my dream. My parents told me, 'Maybe you need to become an oceanographer if you want to become a Captain Nemo.' So I became an oceanographer. Then my parents said, "Maybe you need to become a naval officer," and I did. I used this as my guiding principle, it allowed me to go on and live my dream. I believe all of us have dreams. All of us should try to live our dreams."

Pursuing his, he studied chemistry and geology at the University of California. The outbreak of the Vietnam War saw Ballard called up for active duty in the army. In an inspired move, he transferred to the navy, where he was assigned to the prestigious Woods Hole Oceanographic Research Institute in Massachusetts. His career as an explorer of the seas had begun. After receiving his doctorate in geology and physics from the University of Rhode Island in 1974, there followed a decade of hard graft, in which he spent a third of each year at sea mapping the previously uncharted ocean floor in *ALVIN*, his deep-sea submersible. Then, in his words, he "turned science upside down" in 1977 with the landmark discovery of thermal vents off the Galapagos. All the oceans of the planet, his team found, were recycled through the earth's crust every six million years. More dramatically still, there were living chemosynthetic animals in the dark waters.

"We discovered the first major ecosystem ever found that does not live off the energy of the sun, but the energy of the earth itself. This changes all those thoughts about how life began on our planet. It changes the thoughts about the potential for life on other planets."

But the technology to observe such phenomena was limited. Ballard set about rectifying that. In 1982, he convinced the navy's top brass to fund his research into a fully manoeuvrable, remote-controlled, photographic robot capable of sending back real-time images from the ocean floor. The fruit of his seven years' labours was the Argo-Jason system. To test the equipment as he developed it, he resolved to find the *Titanic*, unseen since she sank to the bottom of the North Atlantic in 1912. Two miles beneath the surface loomed the unmistakable profile of the most famous ocean liner in history, her empty lifeboat davits hanging in the darkness. Ballard's footage that accompanied the find made headlines all over the world. Discoveries of the German battleship *Bismarck* and the liner *Lusitania* soon followed.

Asked by one interviewer what were the goals of exploration, Ballard had his own, suitably inspiring, definition. "To me it's very much like... life is an epic journey and an epic journey you begin with a dream or concept, something crystallises in your mind and then you have to prepare for it. You have to go and assemble your Argonauts to do it. And you have to go forth on the journey and overcome the Cyclops or the Sirens calling you onto the rocks. Every expedition I've ever gone on the Sirens have called me and I tie myself to the mast and I don't listen. You're always tested and then you attain a truth. That's what scientific inquiry is, attaining truths, and then you come back and share that truth with society at large. That releases you and you can go on another journey and I think that that's what exploration is all about and what life is all about and I think that when you do that young people tune in on it. There's a natural frequency to it."

Through his own ground-breaking research Ballard has been able to harness the power of technology to inspire huge numbers of children into scientific exploration through the Jason Project. In 1997, he founded the Institute for Exploration in Mystic, Connecticut in a bold attempt to pioneer a new field of academic endeavour, deep-water archaeology. With Ballard behind the initiative, success was not long in arriving and it was hardly surprising when the largest concentration of Roman ships and the oldest shipwrecks ever seen at such depths were discovered.

In 1996, the National Geographic Society presented him with the Hubbard Medal for "extraordinary accomplishments in coaxing secrets from the world's oceans and engaging students in the wonders of science".

At 63 there are no signs of slowing down. Ballard is president of the Institute for Exploration in Mystic, Connecticut, and an explorer-in-residence at the National Geographic Society. The author of numerous books, scientific papers and magazine articles chronicling his underwater finds, he continues to scour the ocean floor. Recent finds include four 1,500-year-old ships in the Black Sea and the *PT 109*, John F. Kennedy's boat sunk in World War II.

Ballard says he hopes his gravestone will simply say 'Explorer'. But his epitaph will almost certainly concentrate on his most famous discovery. "I still can't get away from finding the *Titanic*. It's going to track me down to the grave."

"You don't know where the envelope is unless you push on it. Most people think they're pushing the envelope, when they're not even close to the envelope. I love taking people who are the best of the best and taking them beyond where they think they can go. You live for those moments."

Robert Ballard

Robert Ballard navigating during the Titanic *search centre, 1985.*

REBECCA STEPHENS

She is the first British woman to have climbed Everest. She is also the first British woman to have climbed the highest peak on all of the world's seven continents. Yet like many men and women between these covers, Rebecca Stephens is not comfortable with the designation of explorer.

First, in her own words, "I haven't been anywhere that people haven't been before," and second,

"I think that the Western world has somehow hijacked the word exploration. We talk about exploration to new places when in fact what we mean is places where white man hasn't been before. Indigenous peoples might have been there for centuries!"

An attractive woman familiar to British television viewers as a former presenter on 'Tomorrow's World', Stephens's background was in journalism rather than science or exploration. Her relish for nature and the outdoors has been a constant since she can remember. She was born in 1961 and grew up in a village just outside Sevenoaks in Kent.

"I've always loved nature, since I was a kid. I didn't know anything about mountaineering when I was young, but when I discovered it some years later it was almost as if something had been rekindled within me. I can remember my happiest moments as a child were on holiday in places like Dartmoor or the Yorkshire Dales. These places definitely sparked something inside me."

Later, as a student working on a farm in Kenya, she recalls a moment of great clarity, the first time she had an awareness of the complete joy of living in the moment. Again, it was all tied in with Mother Nature. "I was supposedly working hard on the farm but I was actually having a wonderful time, getting a taste of a different way of life and exploring the country. There was one moment when I was sitting in the garden of the farmhouse, looking out across the Rift Valley. There were acacia trees dotted across the valley, cattle and horses grazing in the shade of the trees. It was unbelievably beautiful and I sat there, soaking it all in, squeezing a basket full of lemons that I had just picked from the orchard to take with us on safari the following day. I remember at that moment thinking, this is it, perfection."

Perfect it may have been, but at this stage Stephens still had no inkling about which way her life was taking her. She pursued a career in journalism and in 1989, as the 27-year-old deputy editor of a *Financial Times* magazine, landed a tremendous assignment. She was sent to Tibet to cover a mountaineering expedition attempting to climb Everest's North East Ridge. It was here, reporting back to her readers, that the mountaineering flame was kindled. As a late starter, she understood the need to get on with it and develop her climbing skills. Such was her commitment and focus that it took her little time. Four years later, in 1993, she climbed to the summit of the world's highest mountain and won acclaim as the first British woman to reach the top of the world. As an experienced journalist, her book telling the remarkable story of this ascent – *On Top of the World* – was almost a formality.

Soon, the challenge of Everest completed, she sought a larger quest: to climb the Seven Summits, the highest peaks on all seven continents. After her earlier climbs of Kilimanjaro and Denali came the familiar roll call of Elbrus, Carstensz Pyramid and Aconcagua. One more remained, Mount Vinson in Antarctica. In November 1994, when she set foot on its summit and into the record books, she had an emotional, cathartic moment, the highlight of her personal journey of exploration.

"It took me completely by surprise, because Vinson isn't a difficult mountain to climb. It's a little over 16,000 feet – nothing considering I had just come off Aconcagua (23,834 feet) and was well acclimatised. But it was the seventh of my Seven Summits and tears rolled down my cheeks. I didn't know if I was crying out of sheer joy or sadness that it was all over. But there was no questioning that we were in a beautiful place. Standing on the top of that mountain we looked out at a scene that was both rare and lovely: the purest of white snow stretching as far as we could see, with just the very tops of a few mountains protruding above the vertical miles of glacial ice, like islands in a frozen sea. I wanted to jump in a boat and sail to them."

Stephens's restless energy has ensured that life after her seven summits has been no anti-climax. In 1996, she joined forces with polar explorers Sir Ranulph Fiennes and Mike Stroud on an 'Eco-Challenge' race across Canada, riding horses, climbing, white-water rafting, mountain-biking and even hopping into a canoe; and in 2001 she crossed South Georgia in the footsteps of Shackleton. She says the expedition bug has completely caught hold. "It's harder for me now, but if I don't at least travel to somewhere remote, away from the madding crowd, every year or so, I get a bit mournful. It's almost an addiction – I need it to recharge the batteries. And being away for a spell makes me appreciate home more as well."

Stephens also spends time on the motivational lecture circuit. She is a trustee of Sir Edmund Hillary's Himalayan Trust and a regular writer in the travel pages of British newspapers and magazines. She was awarded the MBE in the 1994 New Year's Honours List.

Lord Hunt, leader of the 1953 Everest expedition that put Edmund Hillary and Sherpa Tenzing Norgay on the summit, was a great inspiration for her. She recalls that when Hunt was asked what was the justification for their climbing Everest, he said, "Ultimately the justification will lie in the seeking of their 'Everests' by others, stimulated by this event as we were inspired by others before us... there is always the moon to reach."

Stephens believes, as did Hunt, that everyone has their own 'Everest', whether physical or in the mental or spiritual world.

"The important thing is to first recognise it and then to have the courage to go with it."

"It's about setting sights, taking initiative, overcoming fears and sheer tenacity and grit. And it's about recognising one's limitations and working collectively with other people – about leadership and teamwork. Without the Sherpas, I could never have climbed Everest."

Rebecca Stephens

Ang Passang and Kami Tchering, climbing Everest's South East Ridge with Stephens on her 1993 summit day.

STEVE FOSSETT

Are there any records that are safe from Steve Fossett? Sometimes you have to pinch yourself and wonder. It could be flying, sailing, gliding or even ballooning. Fossett has taken all of them up, one by one, and smashed a series of records in the process. And he hasn't even been doing them that long, either.

He didn't start sailing or ballooning until 1993. Mountaineers must be thankful that at 62 the businessman-turned-adventurer is unlikely to turn his thoughts to swiping a few of their records, too. Or is he?

He was born in Jackson, Tennessee, in 1944 and grew up in California committed to exploring the great outdoors. "It all goes the way back to when I was a Boy Scout," he told *The Explorers Journal* in 2005. "I climbed my first mountain when I was 12 years old with my Boy Scout troop and I continued to pursue mountain climbing as my primary adventure sport."

Record-breaking, adventure and exploration initially took a back seat while Fossett made his fortune as a young man, after gaining his first degree from Stanford in 1966, followed by an MBA from Washington University in 1968. In 1980, he became president of Larkspur Securities, a Chicago-based financial trading company. He has discreetly declined to admit whether he made millions or billions of dollars. Either way, it is the sort of arsenal many explorers would kill for.

Judging by the number of world records he has broken in five different fields – at last count 113 – you might expect Fossett to be an overexuberant, overconfident, noisy individual. In fact, the words most often used to describe him are modest, grounded and unassuming. "Affable and relaxed, Fossett seems less an addict of intrepid abandon than a benevolent manager for whom foresight, planning and the odd spreadsheet are key tools of the trade," wrote a journalist penning a profile for the *Guardian* in 2004.

Adventure started challenging business for primacy in Fossett's life in the 1980s, he says. First up was something that would strike fear and loathing into the heart of many a Briton. "In the 1980s I became interested in extending my adventuring activities into other fields. The first was swimming the English Channel, which was a major challenge because I'm not a very good swimmer, but I finally did succeed in 1985. My two most extensive projects were sailing and ballooning, both of which I started in 1993. I now thoroughly enjoy sailing, especially with a good team. I find it very relaxing to be on the water. Flying an airplane or a balloon I do more as a challenge, rather than something I do for pleasure."

Persistence, a quality whose importance is constantly emphasised in these pages, is a watchword for Fossett. What one sometimes forgets is that his record-breaking attempts have failed on numerous occasions. Each time, however, he picks himself up, dusts himself down, and gets back to the challenge. Nowhere was this truer than in his quest to fly a balloon solo round the world. His first attempt came in 1996, when he only managed to get to

Canada. Four more attempts followed between 1997 and 2001, including a near-death experience in 1998 when his balloon was shredded at 8,800 metres above the Australian coast, sending him plunging into the Coral Sea. Then, in 2002, after seven years of trying, he finally reached his ballooning nirvana with the first solo around the world of 20,626 miles, establishing a round-the-world speed record for good measure. Not without some suitably hairy moments.

"At one point I had to hand-fly the balloon at under 500 feet in order to avoid an adverse wind direction at altitude. A frozen burner control also could have ended the mission when it stuck on full open, but I got through that, too. And during the last night, a small but readily controlled propane fire just added to the excitement... Fortunately I was awake and instantly dove for the tank shutoff valves. I then reconnected the fuel line and tightened it. No problem!"

Casting his eye over an eyebrow-raising list of world records – everything from fastest sail around the world and across the Atlantic to the first solo flight around the world and the longest flight in a glider and many, many more – Fossett is in no doubt as to which is his most important achievement. "It was the first around-the-world solo balloon flight, because the technology did not exist to make a balloon flight of even a fraction of that length when I started the project. The project carried through a period of eight years and six attempts. We did more develop-ment in the balloon flight and worked harder than in any of my other projects."

In 2001, notwithstanding the fact that he had never sailed in the America's Cup, the Volvo Ocean/Whitbread Race, the Olympics or even a world championship event, he was awarded

the prestigious Rolex Yachtsman of the Year at the age of 57, the oldest recipient in its 41 years. The judges were simply unable to overlook his serial record-breaking on the water. His Round The World Record of 58 days 9 hours in 2004, since broken, and the transatlantic record of 4 days 17 hours in 2001 – which still stands – were both huge improvements over the previous records. From 1993, when he took up sailing, to 2004, he set a staggering 23 official world records. Whatever adventures he pursues, he harnesses the power of the very latest technology to achieve them.

"They are all about taking the latest technology and making the most of it, building and sailing the fastest sailboat, maximising the potential of the fastest airplane, developing and testing the technology to fly a balloon around the world – and, of course, meeting the challenge of harnessing weather systems to make these records possible."

Early 2006 saw Fossett in unrelenting form, determined to make the longest flight in the history of aviation – and he succeeded with a non-stop flight of 41,467 kilometres (25,766 miles) ending on 11 February 2006. He says:

"I consider myself to be an adventure sportsman, but I also like to think of myself as an explorer. I am involved in taking on challenges that are personally interesting to me and that are the premier challenges in each of the fields that I have chosen."

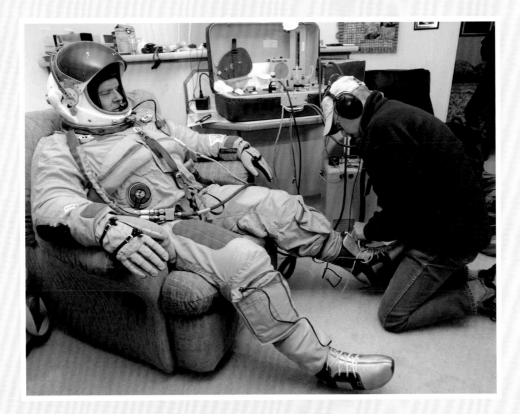

*"I do this as a matter of personal satisfaction. To achieve something that is difficult and
that stretches my ability to do it."*

Steve Fossett

*American adventurer Steve Fossett has his pressure suit adjusted by technician Mike Todd during
a test fitting at the Perlan Project workshop, Omarama, 24 July 2002.*

MIKAEL STRANDBERG

Had it not been for a couple of Jack London novels and a bout of measles as a boy, Mikael Strandberg may never have made it as an explorer. The 10-year-old Swede, laid up, bored and with time to kill, got his hands on the classic novels **White Fang** *and* **The Sea Wolf***, which his working-class father had on permanent loan from the local library as a defiant demonstration of the family's upwardly mobile aspirations.*

They were the only two books in the house. Reading them led to Strandberg's first significant discovery. Suddenly, he had crossed into "an unknown, very exciting and important world", which gave him "self-confidence and a sense of uniqueness", the knowledge that "my future lay beyond the limits of the village."

Way, way beyond them, in fact, as his later expeditions would prove beyond doubt. Born in 1962 in Dala-Järna, he was disillusioned by what he calls the "the utterly boring knowledge taught in school" and at 16 hightailed it for India to spend a year studying Mahayana Buddhism, a fruitless intellectual quest that resulted only in "diarrhoea and gut pains". He says his early desire to "build bridges of understanding between people by writing, lecturing, filming and through photography" not surprisingly "met a total lack of interest". He needed to do something remarkable to find his voice.

Enter the bicycle, a vehicle on which Strandberg would pedal his way out of provincial anonymity onto the world stage of high-spirited adventure. Pondering Strandberg's journeys on two wheels, above all the sheer scale of them, makes conventional distances wither away into insignificance. How about his first one, for instance, a two-year, 17,000-mile bicycle ride from Chile to Alaska which he began in 1986 at the age of 24. Most people would get sore legs just thinking about it.

He followed that auspicious debut with an even longer trip, a 21,000-mile journey from the North Cape of Norway down through Europe and Africa to Cape of Agulhas, the southernmost point of Africa. Gruelling it may have been, but it had the entirely unexpected benefit of introducing him to his future wife. Returning to Sweden halfway through the trip for medical reasons, he was doing a radio phone-in when a woman called Titti called in. "On a live broadcast she asked me out for dinner and I could not say no," Strandberg remembers. "After our dinner I immediately returned to Africa to finish my journey. In love with this woman."

His third great bicycle journey was from New Zealand to Cairo, another mammoth two-and-a-half-year, 18,000-mile expedition. By now, Strandberg was well known, a familiar face to Swedish television viewers.

For Strandberg, exploration is a key to unlocking the biggest mystery of them all. He says,

"I explore to understand the meaning of life.
I am looking for an answer regarding the eternal

question, why on earth did we humans end up on earth, dominating it the way we do, but not fully understanding it. And I believe that to be able to understand fully, you have to understand the basic values of people who live very close to nature every day of their lives."

His quest for such elusive answers took Strandberg, accompanied by Titti, to Patagonia and then Tanzania on journeys that became high-profile films and books. In 2005, Strandberg, then 43, completed a year-long 2,200-mile expedition along the Kolyma River from south to north, traversing a section of north-eastern Siberia so remote no Western explorers had ever ventured there. Mapping this virgin territory and meeting settlers and indigenous peoples along the way, Strandberg and his partner Johan Ivarsson had to survive temperatures as low as minus 58 degrees Celsius, so cold, according to Strandberg, that it can "freeze the liquid behind your knees and elbows".

The happiest moment of his career, he says, was the moment he and Ivarsson arrived in Kolymskaya towards the end of their expedition. It was a blissful farewell to hauling 660lb of kit in darkness and impossibly cold conditions. The entire population of the settlement trooped out to welcome them with hugs and local delicacies.

"After having survived mainly on moose meat and raw, frozen fish during most of the winter, we nearly cried when we came across big plates of fried reindeer brain and cooked bone marrow," Strandberg says. "At that stage, I suddenly realised, after spending 20 years of exploring extreme parts of our world and trying to understand the meaning of life, from now on, I'll stop thinking about the big worrisome issues and simply concentrate on the uncomplicated ones. Like the thought of some more cooked bone marrow."

Strandberg sees himself as a bridge-builder between cultures, his mission "to get people in my own world to understand other people, for them unknown and often misunderstood". He says to work effectively in this field it is important to have a solid base. "By that I mean that even at home it is important to take one's social responsibility in your own community. For me that means that I have founded some society activities, but due to lack of time I have had to close some of them."

Contemplating the future of exploration, Strandberg is filled with foreboding. "There's an awful lot of young male-dominated quite ridiculous adventures today, where focus is purely on showing off a male hero image," he argues. "The type who's gone to the North Pole and back sitting in a shopping cart from Wal-Mart using an oar to move forward and keep polar bears at bay. A bloke whose selling point is dirty underwear, ice in his beard and modern polar clothes packed with sponsors and whose lecture theme is 'Everything is possible!'. I hope this awfully trivial way to travel in the name of exploration will disappear soon and I look forward to the return of good old exploration in the name of documentation, building bridges of knowledge whilst doing research and tests of human limits."

"Even though the majority of things have been discovered geographically today, there's an enormous amount of important things still to discover, since the world is forever changing. Don't think, just go. You will make a difference. It is the best life one can imagine. The life of an explorer."

Mikael Strandberg

Mikael and his wife Titti in Maasailand, in the Il-Loitai district, sharing a traditional meal with a local chief.

BENEDICT ALLEN

As a small boy watching his pilot father bring back weaver birds' nests and stuffed crocodiles

from Africa, Benedict Allen determined on becoming an explorer.

It is unlikely he ever envisaged having to eat his dog.

This infamous incident on his first solo expedition in 1983, a six-and-a-half-month trip from the mouth of the Orinoco to the mouth of the Amazon through remote rainforest, won Allen fame and a degree of notoriety. There were mutterings of plagiarism and exaggeration from a clutch of seasoned rainforest explorers who resented the affable young giant's meteoric rise (he is six feet four inches tall). Undeterred, Allen never looked back and since that expedition he has rarely failed to surprise during two decades of exploration immersed in the lives of indigenous peoples in some of the most remote corners of the world.

Born in 1960, he read environmental science at the University of East Anglia. He treated his final year as an opportunity to launch himself into the expedition world, travelling to Costa Rica, Brunei and Iceland.

Travelling solo has always been a defining feature of his journeys. He undertakes expeditions to live among tribes and learn about their environment – and how they adapt to it – from them.

"To me, exploration isn't about planting flags, conquering nature or going where no one's gone before in order to make your mark. It's about the opposite. It's about opening yourself up, making yourself vulnerable, and allowing the place to make its mark on you."

He certainly allowed Papua New Guinea to make its mark on him during a six-month stint after his debut in the South American jungle. It was an expedition which attracted another flurry of attention after he underwent a brutal male initiation ceremony at the hands of the Niowra or 'Crocodile People', which left him scarred for life. Literally. The scarring was followed, for good measure, by six weeks of daily beatings in order to make him, and the other initiates, 'as strong as a crocodile'.

One of his longest journeys was the five-and-a-half-month, 3,000-mile expedition by horse and camel from Siberia across the Mongolian steppe in 1997, climaxing in a lone 1,000-mile crossing of the Gobi Desert. Moving into television, Allen has received greater notice, pioneering a new style of filming without crew, recording some of his most arduous moments in scenes that have horrified and mesmerised British viewers.

He says one of the most exhilarating moments of his career came during his three-and-a-half-month trek by camel across the Namib Desert in 1996, a journey recorded in the BBC series 'The Skeleton Coast'. "I was alone in the Namib Desert with just my three camels, when suddenly we came across some elephants;

The camels hated the elephants, they'd never seen anything bigger than themselves. But for me it was a very special encounter. No one in the world knew where I was exactly and, after tying up the camels, I sat down quietly to spend time alone with these creatures of such power."

In one of his more recent expeditions, a 1,000-mile trans-Siberian journey with huskies in 2000, he brought the extremes of an unusually vicious winter into sitting rooms around the world in his series 'Ice Dogs'. Just watching it made you freeze.

"Exploration, which has evolved rapidly over the past two centuries, will continue to drive us forward in new ways," says Allen. "The time for great land journeys is over. Walking to the poles and so on is now only about sport, and nothing much else. We are only just tackling the deep ocean and underground, but otherwise exploration of the planet is increasingly about science, in ever increasing detail, especially genetics and the investigation of individual species and systems." Here, mankind is only just scratching the surface. "We have named only 1.5 million of this planet's species and there are perhaps ten more – or a hundred, if you include bacteria. One increasingly important field of scientific discovery is the brain, which we have hardly explored at all. But whichever direction exploration leads, there will always be different ways of perceiving the world, so writers – not just scientists – will continue to have a role, examining and reinterpreting our surroundings for our time."

Throughout his career Allen has displayed an unusually strong empathy with the tribes among whom he has lived. He is, perhaps more than most modern explorers and adventurers, keen to bridge cultural divides. A recent television venture took him to Haiti, Indonesia, Mexico and Siberia for his series 'Last of the Medicine Men', in which he probed the intriguing and barely understood world of shamans, witchdoctors and spiritual healers.

Allen's message, in keeping with the spirit of the times, is inclusive. "We are all explorers," he says. "Curiosity is one of the characteristics that defines us as human. So you don't need to go off to some jungle or desert. We are all exploring the world around us daily, whether we are an artist, a nomad in Borneo, or a banker in Zurich. I'd also say that you can do most things in life, if you really, really want. Don't be put off: follow your own True North." It is difficult to imagine his own would ever lead to a career in banking.

One of his most trusted – and unlikeliest – items he travels with is a bunch of postcards of Queen Elizabeth II. He explains,

"I point at her crown, and explain that it's her headdress and that she's my 'headman'. In the Amazon, she went down really well. These postcards help form a bridge between cultures, and show that I'm not so very different from them."

Such protestations aside, Allen is of course very different, both from his fellow Britons and the tribespeople with whom he has spent such a great deal of time. Why else would he be referred to as 'the real-life Indiana Jones' and 'television's most fearless man'?

"To me exploration isn't about conquering natural obstacles, planting flags... It's not about going where no one's gone before in order to leave your mark, but about the opposite of that: about making yourself vulnerable, opening yourself up to whatever's there and letting the place leave its mark on you."

Benedict Allen

Benedict Allen in the Namib Desert, Namib Naukluft National Park, Namibia.

ANDY EAVIS

The British speleologist or cave explorer Andy Eavis displays none of the reticence common to so many explorers about being called an explorer. On the contrary, he is admirably and refreshingly frank about it all.

"I consider myself an explorer before anything else," he says. "I am an explorer before I am a caver really. What turns me on is actually going where no man has ever gone before. Seeing only one set of footsteps behind me is just a brilliant buzz and I would love to have explored continents and countries but it's all been done so the only thing really left within my budget to explore are caves."

For most of us the very notion of caving elicits a reflexive shudder and a frown, conjuring up images of hideously cramped passageways filling with water, a claustrophobic's nightmare. For Eavis, however, "the thrill of going into places where nobody has ever been before... is amazing and is almost a drug", never mind that these places may be hundreds of metres below ground.

And, as Eavis would be the first to point out, subterranean exploration does not have to involve stomach-churning struggles through tiny apertures. He entered the *Guinness Book of Records* – and the explorers' hall of fame – after his discovery of the world's largest cave in 1981, a chamber so big, in fact, that it caused a fellow team member to suffer agoraphobia.

His expedition to the remote jungle of the Gunung Mulu National Park in Sarawak, north of Borneo, resulted in the startling discovery of what was subsequently christened the Sarawak Chamber, a cave that was 2,300 feet long, 1,300 feet across and 230 feet high, three times the size of what was then considered the world's largest cave, in New Mexico. Another way of describing such an enormous space would be to say that it could accommodate 38 football pitches, 10 jumbo jets end-to-end, three of the old Wembley Stadiums or two Millennium Domes.

"I actually came back to Britain virtually the next day and announced to the world that we had found the biggest enclosed space on the planet – so that was good – really exhilarating stuff," he recalls.

Born in Hampshire in January 1948, Eavis read engineering at Leicester University, where he joined the exploration and caving societies. "I immediately found myself in the Yorkshire Dales looking at caves, which I enjoyed the physical challenge of. I was a farming country boy and wallowing around in mud and water didn't worry me at all and I then got head-hunted into a university expedition."

This first expedition, in 1969, took him to Arctic Norway, where he found himself sitting on a glacier for 10 weeks. It was, he says, "spectacular", but characteristically he branched off to do his own thing. "Under the glacier were ice caves so I found myself as a one-man caving expedition in amongst a glaciological expedition, so I explored, surveyed and photographed a number of kilometres of ice cave and really that got me going."

In 1975 he had his first taste of expedition leadership, organising a mammoth six-month 24-person, £80,000 mission to Papua New Guinea. The trip was a success, charting 50 kilometres of new caves.

Though his business focus remained on the plastics moulding company he co-founded in the late 1970s, cave exploration took him repeatedly to the East. He introduced the Chinese to modern caving and, through the China Caves Project, which he led in the UK, made huge progress in discovering and mapping new caving systems over the past two decades in the most important caving area in the world. In recent years, he has turned to several other countries, including under-explored Myanmar.

Contemplating the future of his field, Eavis reckons well under half of the world's caves have been discovered, "so there is another half to explore, but whether anybody finds anything bigger is questionable. I can't say categorically, I was wrong once about the biggest chamber in the world so maybe there will be something bigger than the current biggest. From a rock mechanics viewpoint, it is hard to envisage anything bigger than the Sarawak Chamber because it shouldn't be there, it should have collapsed at that size and it's hard to think of anything that could be bigger, but you never know."

That challenge will fall to the next generation of cavers, for whom Eavis is an inspiring mentor, determined to pass on his skills. He says the motivator for them will be original exploration, which has always been his great passion. "I have just done a trip with three newcomers in their mid-twenties," he says. "They were taken on a trip specifically to encourage younger

people and two out of three of them proved to be enormously successful and their joy of discovering enormous cave passages was brilliant. It was like having children and watching when they first start discovering anything... I actually stopped a piece of gigantic passage exploration and left it to them to do with young eyes and they thought it was just brilliant, absolutely amazing. It changed their lives."

Unsurprisingly, given his long career underground, Eavis has had a number of near-death experiences, most notably in the French Pyrenees in the early 1970s, when he was attempting to prove that the Pierre Saint Martin cave was the world's deepest. A flash flood came close to killing him and his two colleagues. Closer to home a couple of decades later, he was almost buried alive in the Mossdale Cave in the Yorkshire Dales. Not bad for someone who has spent far too much of his life underground. "I shouldn't be around today," he admits.

Eavis certainly doesn't opt for the classically British technique of understatement when it comes to assessing his achievements in the field of exploration. He says,

"It is possible that I have been responsible for the discovery of more unknown places than any other living person."

It is difficult to argue with that.

"I have walked across chambers and passages and seen one set of footprints
behind. That's my own version of Neil Armstrong's famous quote,
'one small step for man, one giant leap for mankind'."

Andy Eavis

First skylight at Chuan Yan, China, 1984.

Sir CHRIS BONINGTON

With his snowy beard and seer-like face, Sir Chris Bonington is Britain's best-known and best-loved mountaineer. A veteran of numerous expeditions to the highest peaks in the world in the 1970s and 1980s, his stellar record in the mountains on all seven continents includes a clutch of notable first ascents.

The urge to get out and explore goes back to his earliest days as a toddler. "I was adventurous from the start," he confesses. "As a very young child, our garden backed on to Hampstead Heath in London, and at the age of three I slipped out of the back gate and went wandering over the Heath. Hampstead Heath became my adventure playground and going on to the hills of Wales, Scotland and finally the Himalayas was just an extension of this."

He was born in 1934 in London, where he grew up and went to school. After passing through the Royal Military Academy at Sandhurst, he flirted with an army career by joining the Royal Tank Regiment but it was a short-lived affair. That dalliance with life in uniform was followed by a foray into the corporate world when he joined Unilever as a management trainee but again, it wasn't for him. He wanted to climb mountains.

"I love going to places where people haven't been before, the excitement of anticipation of a fresh view round the next corner in a valley, over a mountain pass, or from the summit of an unclimbed peak."

In 1962, he threw in the corporate towel to go into mountaineering full-time. He already had something to show for himself with first ascents of Nuptse (7,879 metres) and Anapurna 2 (7,937 metres). The first British ascent of the legendary North Face of the Eiger later that year propelled him to the forefront of British mountaineering. *I Chose to Climb*, published when he was 32, was the first of a series of successful books.

The 1970s and 1980s saw Bonington treat the Himalayas – among other great ranges – like his back garden, roaming freely and bagging a number of first ascents, including Changabang (6,864 metres), Kongur Tagh (7,719 metres), the West Summit of Shivling (6,501 metres) and Ogre (7,284 metres).

His first attempt on Everest came in 1972. He returned three times in his bid to reach the summit, including an ascent of the South West Face in 1975. Ultimately, it was in 1985 that he summited the mountain on which he had seen a number of friends perish. It was an emotional moment.

"I'd been focused on Everest for something like 12 years. The first time I went to the South West Face, it was in 1972 and I finally got to the top in 1985. And I'd lost a lot of friends. I'd worked incredibly hard, been pretty obsessive and in climbing that mountain, I'd got that out of my system. What I've always loved in climbing is actually the exploratory side of climbing, of going with very small groups and just going off and climbing unclimbed peaks or unclimbed routes and that just freed me up to do that. And so there was a sense of relief that I'd finally done it."

He still rhapsodises about the "absolutely incredible" view from the top, how he was able on that fine day to see the full curvature of the earth, the entire chain of the Himalayas to the east and west and the "rounded rolling hills with the occasional snow-capped mountain" of the Tibetan plateau. "It's a wonderful place to be," he remembered on the fiftieth anniversary of the Hillary and Tenzing ascent.

Bonington, a sensitive man whose heart is in the mountains, dislikes any talk of the 'conquest' of these peaks. "I think that's a very dangerous attitude and one that I certainly haven't got. The mountain is not inanimate because it certainly hasn't got a personality or a will. It can be quite a live, moving kind of thing – with its avalanches and the weather and everything else. But the way you climb that mountain, the way you survive on that mountain, is actually to understand it – to actually work with it, to actually become part of it and in doing that there's no point in being angry with the mountain," he says, touching on the spiritual, almost mystic aspect of mountains that climbers experience. "There's no point in being angry with what is done, or people who've lost their lives or anything else. We've all chosen to be there and therefore it's a matter of you accept what the mountain is, you understand what the mountain is – maybe it lets you climb it, maybe it doesn't."

Bonington, whose experiences on some of the highest peaks place him among the most successful mountaineers of the world, does not accept that all the sport's great challenges have gone with the ascent of all 14 eight-thousanders. What remains to be tackled is, "essentially, technical climbing – hard climbing on the peaks of the Himalayas and the greater ranges, not going necessarily for the biggest mountain but going for steep faces, steep ridges, steep unclimbed peaks – climbing them in very

adventurous ways. Climbing in Alpine style, which means that you pack a rucksack at the bottom of the climb and you keep going until you get to the top however many bivouacs it takes. Climbing as hard as possible, climbing very fast, which means you can travel light and move quickly. So that in fact the challenge for climbers is almost limitless. There are still thousands of wonderful challenges for young climbers of the future."

He is, not surprisingly, the holder of numerous awards, including the Founders' Medal of the Royal Geographical Society. Maintaining his reputation for leadership among the mountains, he has served as president of the British Mountaineering Council, the Alpine Club, the Leprosy charity LEPRA, and the Council for National Parks. He was knighted in 1996 for services to the sport.

Ever since he decided to go it alone in 1962, Bonington has stuck to his guns and continued doing what he loves best. It has rarely been easy, but nothing worthwhile generally is. He says,

"People are attracted by risk and it might be to go climbing, it might be to go caving, it might be driving fast cars. It's the adrenalin of risk, it's the challenge of the unknown. To give it a wider connotation, if human kind did not get challenged by risk, we'd probably still be in the caves or probably would have never have got where we were."

"If you dream of doing something, stop dreaming, get out, and make it happen."

Sir Chris Bonington

Approaching the south summit of Everest, B.Myrer Lund and Odd Eliassen

photographed by Chris Bonington.

LIV ARNESEN

How often is it that books ignite a dream of some hard-to-achieve adventure in foreign lands?
Throughout these pages there are stories of explorers who discovered within them a fierce
urge to explore after reading a particular book during their childhood.

For Bob Ballard, it was Jules Verne's *Twenty Thousand Leagues Under the Sea*, for Ellen MacArthur it was *Swallows and Amazons*. The Norwegian polar traveller Liv Arnesen had her own literary moment of discovery at the tender age of eight.

"My father gave me Fridjof Nansen's book about his crossing of the Greenland Icecap, but it was written in Danish/Norwegian so it was too heavy for me," she says. "The day after at the library at school I got the school version of *Skiing to the South Pole*. That's when the dream started, when I was eight years old. My parents remember me reading that book."

Dreams have different periods of gestation and in Arnesen's case it was several decades before she realised these early ambitions. Born in 1953 in Bærum on the outskirts of Oslo, she benefited from her parents' passion for the outdoors in general and cross-country skiing in particular. They were also ardent students of polar history, which kept Arnesen's thoughts of adventures at the end of the world alive and kicking.

"I had this South Pole dream as a bit of a day dream
for years and years. I remember when I was 12 years old
talking with my friends about dreams. They had dreamt
about a nice husband, a classic house and car and I told
them about my dream of skiing to the South Pole."

"They said I couldn't do it and that it was a boys' dream so I thought I was strange. It took me many years before I started to articulate that dream."

Arnesen became a teacher before she turned to exploration, and now has degrees in Norwegian language and literature, history, sports and counselling. In the early 1990s she was marketing director of a polar travel company, a convenient base from which to plan her own assault on the South Pole.

First, however, came the crossing of the Greenland Ice Cap in 1992, the first time a woman's team had achieved it unsupported. In 1994, it was time to check in with the childhood dream. Arnesen staked her claim to a place in polar history by becoming the first woman to ski solo and unsupported to the South Pole, a 50-day expedition of 745 miles. "I was 41 before I did it so you do think the times are right," she says. "The time seemed right when I did it." She told the story of this ground-breaking expedition in her amusingly entitled book *Snille piker går ikke til Sydpolen* or *Nice Girls Do Not Ski To The South Pole*.

The solo expedition also brought a moment of great clarity and an emotional realisation that she was at last taking the path she had long sought. "It happened when I was skiing on my own. I think it was day nine or so and I was coming up to the mountain plateau in Antarctica and everything was sort of working – all the equipment and food – and I thought to myself this is fantastic, I am here and I have had this dream for about 30 years. I still get tears in my eyes when I think about that moment, that moment was the best for me. I still remember that day."

Two years after that expedition, Arnesen turned to the North Face of Everest but was forced to descend 6,200 feet from the summit after suffering altitude sickness. Her next challenge was also her greatest, the crossing of Antarctica, a feat no woman's team had ever managed. After a great deal of searching, Arnesen came across the American polar traveller and fellow former schoolteacher Ann Bancroft, with whom she teamed up for the expedition. Like Arnesen, Bancroft had first thought of the journey across Antarctica as a 12-year-old. Both had also been captivated by Alfred Lansing's famous book *Endurance*, the story of Shackleton's attempt in 1914 to lead an expedition across the great white continent.

Arnesen and Bancroft's goal was also to empower children around the world, harnessing the power of technology to extend the frontiers of the classroom, allowing schools a window on to their private journey across the treacherous terrain through the Internet and via satellite telephone. Their website had an extraordinary 23 million hits and the two explorers received a blizzard of 20,000 messages during the journey.

On 11 February, the two women entered the record books after 94 days and 1,717 miles, the first time a woman's team had crossed Antarctica on foot. Towing 250lb supply sledges, they had endured temperatures as low as minus 35 degrees Celsius with a wind chill of 75 below. Whatever the temperatures, Arnesen joked in an interview after their success, it was still

summer. "This is paradise really," she said. They co-authored the aptly named book *No Horizon Is So Far* and have continued their collaboration by attempting to become the first women to cross the Arctic Ocean in 2005, an expedition that was bedevilled and ultimately frustrated by Russian politics.

As an educator and motivator, Arnesen's message to others is clear.

"Most dreams and most goals can be achieved if you're sincere to yourself and listen to your heart, listen when the blood is running faster in your veins and your heart is beating a little, then it is something that is important to you. Even if it's not time or you don't think it's right just keep it for yourself and one day the time is right and it is your turn."

Arnesen's next challenge is the revisited expedition to cross the Arctic Ocean from Russia via the North Pole and on to Canada.

"When some people hit a wall, they go into a depression. I change the focus;
I think I can do it another way. If you don't try, you can never go forward."

Liv Arnesen

Halfway to the South Pole in 1994.

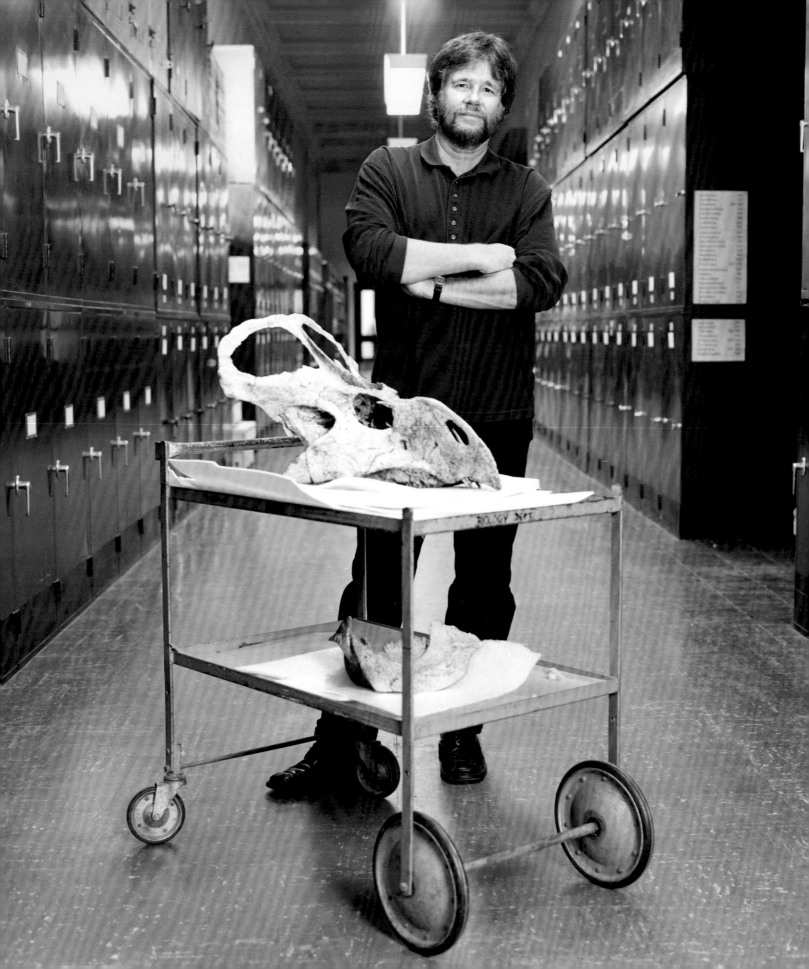

MICHAEL NOVACEK

In layman's terms, he's Mr Jurassic Park, a dinosaur hunter, the man who in 1993 discovered the world's greatest collection of fossils with a team of scientists in the Mongolian Desert. In professional-speak he's the senior vice president and provost of science and curator in the palaeontology division of the American Museum of Natural History in New York.

That's probably not what he envisaged as a guitar-playing, surf-searching, draft-dodging student in 1960s California. Music seemed to be where he was heading. Not that he wasn't interested, at a young age, in rocks and mammals.

"My passion for dinosaurs and other fossils began when I was about seven years old," he once recalled in an interview with *National Geographic.* "I had a book called *All About Dinosaurs* by Roy Chapman Andrews, that was the first of many books that I read and reread on the subject. I was captivated by his account of unearthing dinosaur bones in the Flaming Cliffs of the Gobi, a desert in Mongolia. I vividly remember the drawings of skeletons in the American Museum of Natural History, where I now work, and the etchings of palaeontologists lifting huge dinosaur bones on pulleys.

"My interest wasn't always appreciated by others. When a nun caught me reading about fossils in her class, I was promptly relocated to the section for mystics and dreamers that she called the 'spaceman row'."

These childhood searches were not only literary. Growing up in Los Angeles, the young Novacek, like so many of his fellow explorers in this book, was a wanderer from the start. "I grew up exploring – vacant lots, swamps, later deserts, and caves," he says.

"I can't remember a time when I wasn't driven to do so." His forays into natural history took him across LA on the hunt for frogs, butterflies and alligator lizards.

Had it not been for an impromptu summer field trip to New Mexico as an undergraduate, Novacek would almost certainly not have followed the palaeontology path that led, among other places, right back to the Flaming Cliffs of the Gobi Desert that so captivated him as a child. By now dinosaurs were getting the better of him and he took a doctorate in palaeontology from the University of California in Berkeley in 1978. Within four years he had exchanged west for east by joining the American Museum of Natural History in New York to pursue his fascination with patterns of evolution and the relationships among extinct and living mammals.

Expeditions have taken him all over the world. To Yemen in 1988, where he had a run-in with a bunch of warlords. To the Andes mountains of Chile. To the wilds of Patagonia in the late 1990s. But it is Mongolia which looms largest in Novacek's CV. In 1990, he co-led an expedition to the Gobi, the first Western team to do so since his childhood hero Roy Chapman Andrews in 1922. In 1993, teaming up with the Mongolian Academy of Sciences, Novacek and his collaborators returned, heading into an area known as Ukhaa Tolgod or 'small brown hills'. Once again fate intervened positively. On 16 July, their truck got stuck in the sand and the palaeontologists pitched camp there and then. A few metres above them, incredibly, lying on the ground untouched, were dinosaur skeletons. Further investigation revealed it to be the world's richest site for Cretaceous dinosaurs and other vertebrate animals, the *ne plus ultra* for any palaeontologist. The discovery guaranteed him the sort of profile that has seen him featured in *Time*, *The New York Times*, *National Geographic*, *Newsweek* and a host of other publications. He has even appeared on 'Late Night' with Conan O'Brien, doubtless a first for a onetime President of the Society of Systematic Biologists.

Novacek's skills with a microscope and a shovel are matched by a literary talent that has been widely praised. *Dinosaurs of the Flaming Cliffs*, the story of the Gobi expeditions, was published in 1996. Reviewing his autobiography *Time Traveler* (2002), one critic praised his "ability to write about the most godforsaken places, from Eastern Montana to Mongolia with a sublime gracefulness that makes the reader almost taste the sand and smell the dust."

Sometimes he has to pinch himself at his good fortune earning a living doing what he loves most. "Exploration is more challenging, stimulating, and more fun than most things in life. Looking 'beyond the ranges' is a probe of the unknown, which can be terrifying as well as beautiful, but is always alluring. I am interested in questions of science that consider the history of life on earth. It's fortunate I get to go to many interesting places to find the answers to those questions."

One of those questions concerns extinction. There is no doubt, he says, that humans are responsible for a massive wave of extinction. Population growth and consumption are responsible on one level, but so too is ignorance. Perhaps, it has been suggested, we are our own worst enemy.

"I think we are in that sense because we, as humans, have the capacity to improve the current situation. Yet we have to recognise that our need to do this must take place in spite of some of the other basic needs or urges we might have for more food, more land, more development, more economic growth and so forth. There are lots of good strategies that bring together growth and economics in development with sustainable environment strategies. We don't want to sacrifice everything. Humans have to live. Their lives have to improve. But we have to be more mindful about how that really fits with the environment."

We do not even comprehend the full extent of the damage we are causing earth and its ecosystems, Novacek argues, not least because we don't know the total number of species on the planet, an ignorance he believes has been caused by our predilection for studying the more charismatic species such as whales, lions, tigers, bears and elephants.

Yet Novacek is an American and is, almost by definition, therefore, an optimist. The growing understanding of this biodiversity loss will, he believes, lead us in the right direction, perhaps even before it is too late.

Michael Novacek, during the Mongolian Academy/American Museum
Palaeontological Expedition examining a fossil just collected from the Keerman
Tsav badlands in Mongolia's Gobi Desert.

Mongolia, 2005

GEORGE SCHALLER

For many, he is simply the greatest naturalist of the twentieth century, a man who has spent most of the past 50 years immersed in the wildernesses of Africa, Asia and South America chronicling and helping us understand the mesmerising variety of the planet's wildlife.

He has added vastly to our knowledge of mountain gorillas in Congo, Serengeti lions, Mongolian snow leopards, Chinese pandas and Indian tigers. His travels across the world have always been primed with purpose. Schaller has no time for look-at-me-aren't-I-heroic stunts.

Schaller's understanding of exploration is typically rigorous and scientific. He says,

> *"In its original Latin root the word exploration means to search for, investigate, and understand. For half a century, I have explored the lives of animals, attracted both by their physical realms and intellectual challenges. The more rare and remote a species, whether Tibetan antelope, tiger, or giant panda, the greater the impetus to chronicle its life."*

His uncompromising attitude towards exploration is one which the next generation of publicity-hungry thrill-seekers would do well to heed. "My projects can be considered explorations or even expeditions but not adventures, which to my mind imply poor planning, bad luck, or carelessness. While I pursue a dream and vision with each project and at times pit myself against the elements, I have never just indulged and pleased myself with freak-ish challenges, such as becoming the youngest or oldest to climb a

peak or take the longest pointless trek or sea voyage," he says.

For Schaller, exploration is not about the self. It carries with it an inherent commitment to the wider community, towards improving it in any way, whether through advancing scientific knowledge, preserving the environment, raising awareness or anything else that works to achieve the goal. "I believe that exploration should go beyond self-serving ambition and individual achievement to contribute something to society, to humanity. I admire Sir Edmund Hillary more for his helping Sherpas build schools and health clinics than for his renown of having climbed Mount Everest first. He did not just consume that mountain but extended his personal challenge to create something profound, ethical, and lasting."

George Schaller was born in Berlin in 1933 and moved to Missouri as a teenager. Pursuing his early interest in animals, he studied at universities in Alaska and Wisconsin before becoming a research zoologist at the New York Zoological Society, later renamed the Wildlife Conservation Society.

Published in 1963 when he was just turning 30, his landmark book *The Mountain Gorilla: Ecology and Behaviour* represented a decisive step forward in our understanding of this hitherto little-studied animal, reversing common misperceptions about the gorilla to reveal this was an intelligent, gentle and emotionally sophisticated animal. It also set the framework for a new approach towards animals in their environment, representing the advent of conservation biology. Who knows how many species owe their continued existence to this quiet and shy man? Thanks to Schaller's efforts, the Vietnamese warty pig and Tibetan red deer – both thought extinct – were rediscovered in the mid-1990s.

Thoughtful and articulate, Schaller acknowledges the difficulties in pinpointing exactly the impulse that propelled him into a life of exploration. "What has priority?" he asks rhetorically. "Possible benefits to science and conservation or a seemingly self-indulgent life as a nomadic naturalist partial to wild landscapes and intriguing animals to study, enjoy, and protect? And there is the occasional exhilarating and transcendent experience, as when, for example, a mountain gorilla for the first time approached to sit by me."

He has been as prolific out of the field as in, the author of seminal books including *Serengeti Lion*, *The Last Panda* and *Tibet's Hidden Wilderness*, in addition to hundreds of articles in scientific journals and magazines. Recognising his outstanding achievements in conservation, the World Wildlife Fund awarded Schaller its Gold Medal in 1980. His work in this field has also led to the creation of five wildlife reserves, including the Arctic National Wildlife Refuge in Alaska and the 118,000-square-mile Chang Tang Wildlife Reserve in Tibet.

Working together, science and conservation groups can have a profoundly positive impact on our environment, Schaller insists. He points to the numbers of North American bison, pronghorn and musk ox which have all increased over the past century thanks to such efforts. Highlighting potential financial gains – through the use of ecotourism, for example – can play a part in all this, he acknowledges, but there must be more to it than that or our efforts will be doomed.

"In conservation, the only hope is not economic, it is spiritual. If you can't put a value on something, is it worthless? Can you put a value on a beautiful river? Or a wolf howling? Most people in the world have values beyond economic. And unless you can convince people to think of the spiritual aspects of the environment and what it does for them, you're going to lose it."

These pressures have brought about an expansion in the naturalist's role in society, according to Schaller. Today, to be successful, the naturalist must have sound political skills, not to mention an appetite for fundraising. Through his position within the Wildlife Conservation Society in New York, Schaller remains a highly vocal advocate for his causes. He is currently focused on efforts to protect the last cheetahs in Iran, Tibetan antelope and wild yak on the Tibetan Plateau and Marco Polo sheep in the Pamir Mountains, together with the landscapes in which these species live.

"We all have an obligation to bequeath the earth's beauty to future generations," he argues with conviction. "We must retain wild places in every country where nature can function in all its complexity, variety, and harmony, and where we treat it with respect and compassion. Thus I aspire to an ideal beyond a private sense of merit when I explore the Tibetan uplands, steppes of Mongolia, rainforests of Laos and other parts of the world and that is to help wilderness endure. This challenge will remain with us in the decades and centuries to come."

Without Schaller's pivotal work throughout the twentieth century, one wonders how much more difficult that challenge would be.

"There's too much greed, too much consumption. We have to focus on saving some portion of nature for the next millennium."

George Schaller

Censusing Tibetan Antelope, Kunlun Mountains, Xinjiang, China, July 2005.

ANNA ROOSEVELT

Being the great-grandaughter of a famous American president probably has its moments. Sometimes it's just a drag. Ask Anna Curtenius Roosevelt, the archaeologist and anthropologist who is a direct descendant of Theodore. Journalists often are more mesmerised by Teddy than by archaeology, she thinks.

When, in 1988, she stood inside the Great Hall of the American Museum of Natural History chatting to a reporter after winning the prestigious MacArthur Foundation Fellowship, she was only a few yards away from her ancestor's statue, which graces the museum's front steps. "Why doesn't anyone ever ask me how I'm related to Eleanor, who was the only interesting one in the family?" she wondered aloud. "He gets credit for everything. Remember, he really only went on a couple of safaris, complete with crates of champagne. He's lauded for those few trips because he was a famous president, not because they were important expeditions or because he was a great explorer. It's good to keep things in perspective."

Roosevelt's interest in archaeology goes back a long way. She says it first hit her as a nine-year-old when her mother, grandfather and sisters took her to Mesa Verde, Colorado. "There I saw Esther – a mummy – in the museum, and the cliff dwellings, and artefacts." There were early literary influences, too, a common theme in this book. "I also read a children's book based on Roy Chapman Andrews's Gobi Desert expedition and C. W. Ceram's *Gods, Graves, and Scholars*," she says. "What I liked about Andrews's book was the way the dried-up, red soil with broken chips of dinosaur egg could be interpreted to give a vivid picture of a cool swamp where a mother dino brooding over her eggs was attacked by a predator, supposedly. Ceram's book intrigued me as a child because of the story of the Rosetta stone and its role in the decipherment of Egyptian hieroglyphs."

Growing up in family of women – her father was killed in a plane crash when he was 29 – she credits her mother with fostering and inspiring her love of archaeology. Together the family would go on nature searches looking for arrowheads. The women in her family were also independent-minded and fearless travellers, she says, a quality she has evidently inherited and one which has facilitated her researches in the heart of the Amazonian jungle and in the Congo Basin.

On graduating from Stanford with honours in 1968, she moved to the University of Pennsylvania, where she had her first serious brush with gender bias when her male adviser declared she should not go into the field in the summer break. Undeterred, she left and was accepted at Columbia University but had to leave her Ford Foundation Fellowship behind as a result and got a curator job at the Indian Museum to make ends meet. The museum job became a backdrop for her research as a project leader and a base for successful fundraising. Her dissertation on Venezuelan prehistory received an award of distinction. Then, in 1985, after 15 years, she was fired – the day after returning from a dig in Brazil – for penning a critical, whistle-blowing report on the museum's management to the US attorney general, who was investigating the museum's board.

In the early 1980s, Roosevelt began work in the Brazilian Amazon. After her book on prehistoric moundbuilders and the discovery of 8,000-year-old pottery at Taperinha, published in *Science*, her greatest discovery came at the cave Pedra Pintada, where she unearthed – literally – the remains of spearheads, carbonised fruits, mussel shells and fish bones, together with drops of red pigment used to decorate the interior. Chemical analysis and 53 dates from a cross-section of dating methods led to Roosevelt's thrilling conclusion that the site had been occupied between 11,000 and 10,000 years ago, turning Amazonian anthropology on its head. New discoveries tend to ruffle feathers – think of Marie Tharp in these pages – and this was no exception. The North American archaeologists were upset to have their Paleoindian Clovis culture demoted from father culture to brother and argued for a later dating.

Anthropologists had long maintained that people entered the Amazon Basin only in the recent geological period, not the Pleistocene. Published in *Science* in 1996, her findings infuriated a number of colleagues. One even suggested she was a controversialist with a penchant for stirring things up. The debate rages on, but other archaeologists have made finds comparable to Roosevelt's elsewhere in South America. The different cultures she found and dated in the Amazon form an unprecedented sequence of human development not even guessed at by archaeologists when she started work.

Roosevelt's energy is prodigious, her work-rate formidable. At 24 pages her CV is the longest this author has ever seen, a daunting list of accomplishments, grants, publications, appointments and awards. Today she is a Professor of Anthropology at the University of Illinois at Chicago and a Fellow of the American Academy of Arts and Sciences.

She is a great believer in the symbiotic relationship between archaeologists and indigenous peoples. "Archaeologists need indigenous peoples for their skill and knowledge in their cultures. On the other hand, indigenous people need archaeologists to show how their earlier ancestors lived," she says. "In Amazonia, for example, the Kayapo chiefs were fascinated in our results from digging in the mounds of Marajo Island because it showed them a rich culture that had not previously been strongly linked to them. They said to me about the Marajoara culture, 'This is fantastic. This is our ancestral culture.' Archaeologists and native people together, also, can document how people interacted with environments over the long term."

Archaeology has always been a powerful medium of exploration for Roosevelt.

"I like the process of research and discovery. I love settling down in an archive or museum collection to see what's there and what it might mean, I love following the trail of an idea, searching for sites. Survey is one of the great experiences. Perhaps most satisfying is the process of digging for days, weeks, and months, searching to understand the layers and objects. And I love the drama and suspense of waiting for the radiocarbon dates to be run to find out what the history of the site was."

Some of her colleagues probably tremble at the prospect.

Anna Roosevelt, Brazilian archaeologist Mauro Imazio da Silveira, Carlos Barbosa
and Jose Maria de Sounza at Curupite in the Curua River, an underwater site where a
Paleoindian harpoon point was recovered by miners.

Xingu, Brazil, 2001

ADRIAN COWELL

In the modern era of instant documentaries and 'Big Brother' reality shows, the film-maker Adrian Cowell already seems an anachronism. A product of a more thoughtful, less rushed age, he would be the first to acknowledge this. In an interview he once described himself and the environmental films he helped pioneer over four decades as endangered species.

He was born in China in 1934 and, on leaving Cambridge University, virtually stumbled into documentary film-making. Unusually, there was no inner fire, no compelling vision of the direction he should take. Cowell's path was, instead, an exercise in serendipity that began after landing a role on a university expedition filming in Burma in 1955-56. He crossed paths with a young BBC producer who would become the most famous naturalist on British television.

"I went on an Oxford and Cambridge expedition to the Far East and I had nothing to do with the making of the film but when I came back everyone was too busy to go and help David Attenborough, who was the producer who'd given us £200 – even then it was a tiny amount of money – to make the films. I went and made three films with David and in terms of popularity nothing I have done since has been so successful! So I got into it by accident, and really everything I do has been by accident. Nothing particularly drives me."

The experience spurred a lifelong interest in both film and Burma. A year later, he headed west on another Oxbridge expedition, this time to the rainforest of Brazil. Once again, the experience resulted in a lifelong passion which he went on to explore, memorably, in film.

Discount Cowell's modesty for a moment. For a man who claims to lack the sort of drive that animates most of the explorers in this book, he has, in fact, been enormously successful, winning three British Academy Awards for his ground-breaking, often uncomfortable, films.

Though he is better known for his work in the Amazon, he has also spent a considerable part of his career on the other side of the world, exploring the illegal drugs trade. His early forays in the Far East showed him the damage caused by the industry, notably in Burma, where he started documenting it from the early 1960s, travelling to remote areas with guerrilla groups. He had a close shave or two, once having to extend a six-month trip by a year, hotly pursued by the Burmese army and the Kuomintang, one of the biggest drug-smuggling organisations. "That was quite a relief to get out of there," he chuckles. "We were very, very lucky to get out alive." His travels in Burma resulted in an acclaimed series of films: *The Opium Trail* (1966), *The Opium Warlords* (1974), *Opium* (1978) and *Heroin Wars* (1996). He regards the war on drugs as a farce.

The Decade of Destruction, his seminal documentary on the devastation of the Amazon, was filmed over 10 years during the 1980s. It is rightly regarded as a landmark series, horrifying viewers with the slash-and-burn rape and settlement of a formerly pristine environment. Such was the breadth, depth and authority of its coverage that it generated international debate on rainforest preservation. The future of the Amazon has not left the environmental agenda ever since. In the early 1980s, he remembers, there were no NGOs active in Amazonia. Today there are "half a dozen in every town".

"When I first entered the Amazon, nobody could conceive it to be under threat," he recalls of his earliest experiences. "It threatened us. It was called the 'Green Hell', which of course is nonsense, but that's what it was called. It was inconceivable that man could have any effect on this enormous sort of planetary power which Amazonia was. Now everybody is struggling to protect the last remnants that are left." That they are owes much to the passionate outrage *The Decade of Destruction* engendered.

The same could be said of the peoples of this threatened wilderness. Cowell has dedicated much of his life to preserving their integrity. He considers two of the men he encountered in these efforts as the only true explorers he has ever known.

"Exploration means to me what it did to Livingstone so I don't feel that I'm living in an exploring age. The only genuine explorers I've come across in my career were Orlando and Claudio Villas-Boas who worked for the Brazilian government," he explains. "They were asked to build a chain of airstrips across the southern Amazon because a lot of planes coming down from America were crashing during World War II and so they did a long, ten-year expedition going across these areas. The southern Amazon had been opened up before then by people going down rivers but no one had really crossed between the rivers."

In fact, the trails made by the Villas-Boas brothers became roads which in time led inexorably to deforestation. They sought to compensate for the damage by championing the rights of native Indians through refuges to protect them in the face of expanding settlement, logging and mining operations.

In *The Heart of the Forest*, published in 1961, Cowell evoked his relationships with the Amazonian Indians and how he learnt to live and hunt with them, all the while chronicling the terrible bloodletting between them and the *seringueiros* or Brazilian rubber-tappers. *The Tribe that Hides from Man*, which accompanied his television series of the same name in 1973, told the story of his quest to find the Kreen-Akrore tribe with the Indian Protection Service of the Brazilian government. It illustrated the delicate ambiguity of contacting remote peoples for the first time. The world was witnessing "the very last stages of primary globalisation, the absorption of humans who resist all contact with our global society", Cowell suggested.

Having observed significant environmental degradation in the course of his own lifetime, he now cautions against travel for its own sake.

"Our problem now is, how is the world going to survive if global warming keeps going on? The message is to discourage unnecessary travel. If someone goes from Solihull to the South Pole, well, that's good for him, but it's probably not particularly good for the South Pole or anywhere else."

Panara, Amazon: canoeing down river past Kreen-Akrore fish traps and rapids. The expedition to the Kreen-Akrore tribe, as they were then known, set out in 1968. Panara is the tribe's name for themselves, and once they were contacted, the name Kreen-Akrore ceased to be used.

Panara, Amazon, 1968

Dame JANE GOODALL DBE

No wonder that Jane Goodall believes that "If you really want to do something, work hard and never give up, you will find a way. Follow your dreams." It is a maxim by which she has lived all her life and it has guided her through a truly astonishing career.

That she has succeeded without formal education (for most of her life) in what has traditionally been a jealously guarded preserve of largely male scientists makes her pioneering studies of chimpanzees doubly remarkable.

Goodall was born in London in 1934 and grew up on the south coast in Dorset. Passionate about wildlife, she spent a good deal of her childhood outdoors. Indoors she was hooked on the Tarzan stories and *The Jungle Book,* which gave her the first feel for Africa and the jungle. Even as a tiny child her interest in animals was singular. This is when she really got started, she says.

"I think it was when I hid for four hours in a hen house at the age of four-and-a-half to see how a hen laid an egg! But also a book I was given – *The Miracle of Life* – it was for adults and I was about seven. But it was amazing – details of animals, their structures, what they were for, the habitats, plant life, history of medicine – i.e. discovery of anaesthetics, penicillin etc. Exploring the animal world, the universe, and the human body – all was possible in its pages."

Her mother Vanne provided constant encouragement, never challenging her daughter's aspiration to follow her heart and work with animals in Africa, whatever the difficulties. In 1957, invited to Africa by a friend, she made what was almost akin to a pilgrimage to meet the famed anthropologist and palaeontologist Dr Louis Leakey. He recognised steel and determination and was so impressed by the young Englishwoman he picked her to carry out a pioneering study of chimpanzees in Gombe National Reserve, Tanzania, in 1960. It was a part of Africa that was to become her home. She once said,

"I think a forest is really my spiritual home.
So, when I came to Gombe, I really was home.
It's a world that doesn't change in a world of change.
It's my spiritual anchor."

Leakey thought the study would take at list 10 years; Goodall thought three. In the event it has lasted five decades!

How to study animals that wouldn't let humans get anywhere close? It was a problem that proved infuriating and immensely discouraging in the first weeks. Eventually, Goodall found herself an observation point in a place she christened the Peak. It was from this spot she made two profoundly important discoveries. The first was that chimpanzees ate meat, as she observed the soon-to-be-famous chimp she had named David Greybeard gobbling up a baby bush pig in a tree. Hitherto chimps had been thought of as herbivores with an occasional modest foray into the carnivorous world through eating bugs. The second discovery, perhaps even more startling in its implications, followed only weeks later. Once again it was David Greybeard who provided Goodall – and the world – with the news. She observed him fashioning a tool from a broad blade of grass with which to dig a termite mound. Toolmaking had always been considered a uniquely human skill. This was the first recorded instance of another species doing it and it radically altered our understanding of an animal which shares 98 per cent of our DNA.

Against her instincts she was persuaded by Leakey to gain a professional qualification – a wrench that took her from her beloved chimps – and received her doctorate from Cambridge in 1965, a rarity given her lack of undergraduate degree.

Seminal books accompanied Goodall's researches as she steadily developed into the world's leading primatologist. *In the Shadow of Man* (1971), *The Chimpanzees of Gombe* (1986) and *Through a Window* (1990) were translated into numerous languages and made household names of the Gombe chimpanzees, so much so that when the great matriarch Flo died in 1972 her obituary was printed in *The Times*.

In 1977, she founded the Jane Goodall Institute to support research at Gombe and to protect chimps and their environment more generally, an initiative that still complements the work of Roots & Shoots, a programme she set up in 1991 to encourage children to learn about wildlife and environmental conservation.

"This kind of feeling of responsibility towards the environment or towards animals and people is something, which, unless it's ingrained in children, is a very hard thing to do," she explains. "That's why I'm so passionate about Roots & Shoots. It's about compassion, it's about love, it's about making the world around you a better place. And, if we can get this around the world into groups of children, then the world will be a better place."

During her career some scientists have been sniffy about her insistence on naming rather than numbering the animals she studies, accusing her of anthropomorphising the chimps. Yet she has no inclination to eye her subjects through a cold and dispassionate lens. "Thinking back over my life, it seems to me that there are different ways of looking out and trying to understand the world around us. There's a very clear scientific window. And it does enable us to understand an awful lot about what's out there. There's another window... through which the wise men, the holy men, the masters of the different religions look as they try to understand the meaning in the world. My own preference is the window of the mystic."

Goodall has been serially honoured around the world. She has received the prestigious Kyoto Prize from Japan, the National Geographic Society's Hubbard Medal, among many, many other awards. In 2002, UN Secretary-General Kofi Annan named her a 'Messenger of Peace' and in 2004 she was made a Dame Commander of the British Empire.

"Chimpanzees have given me so much," she says. "The long hours spent with them in the forest have enriched my life beyond measure. What I have learned from them has shaped my understanding of human behaviour, of our place in nature." They have been her great exploration.

"*Thinking back over my life, it seems to me that there are different ways of looking out and trying to understand the world around us. There's a very clear scientific window. And it does enable us to understand an awful lot about what's out there. There's another window... through which the wise men, the holy men, the masters of the different religions look as they try to understand the meaning in the world. My own preference is the window of the mystic.*"

Dame Jane Goodall

Jane Goodall records her chimpanzee observations in her journal by the light of a kerosene lantern in her simple tent, Gombe National Park. Northern Tanzania, 1972.

F. STORY MUSGRAVE

Challenger *(1983 and 1985),* **Discovery** *(1989),* **Atlantis** *(1991),* **Endeavour** *(1993),* **Columbia** *(1996). The astronaut Story Musgrave's CV reads like the history of the space shuttle programme. Which is exactly what it is. And then some, as they say. These days the astronaut describes himself as an artist and a storyteller, something of a poet, too.*

To suggest Franklin Story Musgrave is an unusual man is an understatement of epic proportions, rather like opining that Neil Armstrong's setting foot on the moon was quite an interesting development.

His background confirms the Musgrave family's predilection for the out of the ordinary. High achievement and tragedy go hand in hand. Ancestors include a Supreme Court Justice and a famous nineteenth-century sculptor, but a history of mental illness runs alongside, too. Suicide deprived Musgrave of both parents, his younger brother and a son. His great-grandfather and grandfather had done the same thing. As if that were not enough calamity to fall on one man, Musgrave's older brother was killed in a navy flying accident.

He was born in Massachusetts in 1935 at the height of the Great Depression, growing up on a 1,000-acre dairy farm which brought him into contact with two of what would become his great juxtaposed loves: machinery and nature. He immersed himself in both to escape his difficult family surroundings, characterised by alcoholism and abuse, pootling about fixing farm machinery and romping across fields, woods and hills.

Looking back on a childhood that would have shattered many

lesser men and women, he says it acted instead as a force for good. "Those unbelievable tragedies are what built me. I look back upon them as my Rock of Gibraltar, strangely enough," he told the American Academy of Achievement.

"I think there are huge lessons there, for young people who are getting started in life, as well as other people. And that is, to take responsibility for your own life. Only you are responsible for the course you take from there. You cannot say, 'I went through this,' or 'I have this in my background, therefore I have a right to be unsuccessful, or a right to fail.' If you want to, fine, do that. But no matter what went on, you do have responsibility for the direction of your own life."

As a child there was no single book that inspired Musgrave to a life among the stars, no single outside influence which steered him that way. "Space is a calling of mine, it struck like an epiphany. That occurred when NASA expressed an interest in flying people who were other than military test pilots. And when I was off in the Marine Corps in Korea, I had not graduated from high school yet and so I could not fly. And so I was not a military test pilot, but as soon as NASA expressed an interest in flying scientists and people who were not military test pilots, that was an epiphany that just came like a stroke of lightning. And I saw that everything I had ever done in life could be used in that endeavour. It just fit and it felt just right."

It was hardly the easiest path to choose. Anything but. There were 4,000 applicants for 11 positions. But dedication, talent and persistence tend to pay off. Musgrave was one of the 11.

By the time he applied to NASA, his résumé was little short of outstanding. But it was beginning to look as if he was the permanent student. During a stint in the Marines from 1953 he trained as an aviation electrician and instrument technician, which got him postings as an aircraft crew chief in Korea, Japan and Hawaii. His first Bachelor of Science degree, in mathematics and statistics, came from Syracuse University in 1958. Next came an MBA in business administration and computer sciences at UCLA. Third up was a Bachelor of Arts degree in chemistry from Marietta College, Ohio, rounded off with a doctorate in medicine from Columbia University in 1964. In 1966, unable to kick the degree bug, he completed a Masters degree in physiology and biophysics (in later years he has added further degrees in literature, philosophy, psychology and history).

NASA can be forgiven for not knowing what to make of the young man. "They almost didn't take me because they said I was so over-trained that I might not be comfortable. Apart from everything else that I was doing in life I had about six earned degrees at that time, an active laboratory and a surgical practice, and was a commercial pilot, flight instructor and parachutist."

Yet NASA proved the perfect fit, Musgrave the perfect astronaut. In a NASA career of 30 years, he threw himself into the pioneering Apollo programme, worked on the design and development of the Skylab space station and, from the mid-1970s, led the way in designing extra-vehicular activity equipment including space suits and life support systems for the space shuttle programme. He had to wait 16 years until he flew to space.

Ultimately, he flew six times on the space shuttle, more than anyone else, logging 1,281 hours 59 minutes, 22 seconds in space, in addition to around 25 million miles in orbit. Add that to the 18,000 hours in 160 different types of civilian and military aircraft as pilot, instructor and acrobatics specialist, plus over 600 private parachute jumps, including over 100 of what he calls "experimental free-fall descents to study human aerodynamics".

These days it is through poetry that Musgrave expresses his fascination with the enduring questions of humanity and our place in the universe. It remains the ultimate exploration. This poem, written in 1988, is called '*Story's Prelude*'.

> *The seeds of clover were sown,*
> *the kernels of my soul were grown.*
> *Grew I through food and fear,*
> *through Nature's land far and near.*
> *Grew I, rooted in hill and vail,*
> *till uprooted, born by road and rail.*
> *Among the mountains and the streams,*
> *in and out of all the earthly seams,*
> *up and down the heavenly beams,*
> *melted, molded I by myriad steams.*
> *Sculptured by the seasons,*
> *listening to Nature's reasons,*
> *Grew I, rooted in the ether.*

"Getting out of the comfortable path, that's what exploration is all about."

Story Musgrave

Earth over astronauts. In the earth's orbit, astronauts Story Musgrave and Jeffrey Hoffman
release the Hubble Space Telescope from the cargo bay of the space shuttle Endeavour after
completing repairs, 9 December 1993.

WADE DAVIS

"There are spiritual adventures, physical adventures, geographical adventures, adventures of the heart,"

says Wade Davis, the tousle-haired anthropologist, botanical explorer, photographer and bestselling

author. "But for something to be adventurous it has to be unpredictable."

Davis knows a lot about adventure and a good deal, too, of unpredictability. His whole life has embraced both. He has been a park ranger, a logger, a big game hunting guide, a forestry engineer, writer and broadcaster. His scientific interests mirror the stunning variety of the world's peoples and environments and have included subjects as diverse as Haitian voodoo, the ethnobotany of South American Indians, the traditional use of psychotropic drugs and the global biodiversity crisis.

Along the way he has collected a clutch of degrees, in anthropology and biology with a doctorate in ethnobotany from Harvard. Armed with these professional qualifications, he has become an eloquent and outspoken advocate for the preservation of the world's languages and cultures, increasingly threatened by the rolling tide of globalisation.

"It's neither change nor technology that threatens the integrity of the ethnosphere," he said in an interview with *National Geographic News.* "It is power, the crude face of domination. In every instance, these societies are not failed attempts of modernity. They're not archaic, destined to fade away. They are dynamic, living, vital cultures that are being driven out of existence by identifiable external forces. Whether it is diseases that have come into the homeland of the Yanomami in Brazil, or the fact that the Ogoni in the Niger Delta find their once-

fertile soils poisoned by effluent from the petroleum industry, or whether in Sarawak the forest homelands of the Penan have been destroyed, there is always an identifiable element. This is both discouraging and encouraging, for if human beings are agents of cultural destruction, we can also be facilitators of cultural survival."

Davis offers a refreshing perspective in a world which has come to worship unthinkingly at the altar of Mammon. He provides a powerful antidote to the infection common in the West that our societies are inherently superior to those from less 'developed' parts of the world. Listening to what he has to say makes one realise the West should engage in a little less hubris and a little more humility.

"If you measure success by technological achievement, we're at the top of the heap, but if you were an anthropologist from Mars, you wouldn't rate our social structure so highly. Americans revere marriage, children and grandparents, but half of all marriages end in divorce, our children spend too little time with us because we're working 24-7, and only 6 per cent of grandparents live in the same home as their grandkids. We are consuming at a rate that's not sustainable. Is this the paragon of humanity?"

Born in British Columbia in 1953, Davis enjoys triple citizenship, of Canada, Ireland and the US, somehow apposite in a man who has appreciated cultural diversity more than most. He has spent more than three years in the Amazon and Andes, living with 15 different tribal groups in eight South American countries, amassing 6,000 botanical collections in the process, a figure that recalls the nineteenth-century heyday of botanical exploration.

Today there are around 6,000 different languages spoken in the world, he says, but in a generation around half will disappear because they are not being passed down. "What this means is that we are living through a period of time in which, within a single generation or two, by definition half of humanity's cultural legacy is being lost... Whereas cultures can lose their language and maintain some semblance of their former selves, in general, it's the beginning of a slippery slope towards assimilation and acculturation and, in some sense, annihilation." Language matters and matters enormously. "Language isn't just a body of vocabulary or a set of grammatical rules; it's a flash of the human spirit, the vehicle through which the soul of each particular culture comes into the material world."

People listen to Davis, not least because he is a rare breed: an academic who has also proved able to tap into popular culture with prodigious success. His 1986 book *The Serpent and the Rainbow*, one of 10 he has published, was an international bestseller, delving into the mysterious societies of Haitian voodoo, zombies and magic to critical acclaim. It was later adapted and made into a film. Another landmark publication was *One River: Explorations and Discoveries in the Amazon Rain Forest*, published in 1996. He is equally at home lecturing at institutions such as the American Museum of Natural History, the Smithsonian, RGS and the Explorers Club as he is appearing on television and in the pages of *Newsweek*.

A research associate of the Institute of Economic Botany of the New York Botanical Garden, he is also a board member of the David Suzuki Foundation and Cultural Survival, organisations which accord with his efforts to promote conservation-based development and the protection of cultural and biological diversity. One of his most recent awards is the highly coveted position of National Geographic Explorer-in-Residence, an accolade he shares with several others in this book, including Sylvia Earle, Bob Ballard and, formerly, Jane Goodall. As if these accomplishments were not enough, he is also a talented photographer who has exhibited widely.

Understandably, he gives short shrift to the notion that it is no great loss if indigenous cultures disappear. "Some people say: 'What does it matter if these cultures fade away?' The answer is simple. When asked the meaning of being human, all the diverse cultures of the world respond with 10,000 different voices. Distinct cultures represent unique visions of life itself, morally inspired and inherently right. And those different voices become part of the overall repertoire of humanity for coping with challenges confronting us in the future. As we drift toward a blandly amorphous, generic world, as cultures disappear and life becomes more uniform, we as a people and a species, and earth itself, will be deeply impoverished." However tough the challenges, however powerful the threat, his efforts have helped ensure global biodiversity is firmly fixed on the international agenda.

*"There are spiritual adventures, physical adventures, geographical adventures, adventures of the heart.
But for something to be adventurous, it has to be unpredictable."*

Wade Davis

Sarawak, 1989

Sir CHAY BLYTH

In a nation of inveterate sailors he is among the greatest it has ever produced. For the best part of four decades he has kept the British public, and much of the rest of the world, hooked with his trailblazing adventures on the high seas. His face today is synonymous with British sailing.

What first brought him to public notice was his 1966 brave-the-elements expedition when he rowed across the Atlantic in an open boat with John Ridgeway, ten years before Ellen MacArthur was born. The now legendary journey took the pair 92 blistery days from Cape Cod to the Aran Islands. Blyth's reward, apart from the stupendous heroe's welcome, was the British Empire Medal.

Looking back on it now, Blyth sees this early foray across the seas as emblematic of an opportunity seized.

"All of these things are really to do with opportunities. That was an opportunity and we took advantage of it. That is the key – to recognise these opportunities and to take advantage of them rather than just bumbling along. It's easiest enough to have the opportunity presented to you. It's the taking advantage of it."

Blyth was born in the Scottish town of Hawick in 1940, the youngest of five girls and two boys. He left school at 15 and went to work for a local knitwear factory as an apprentice frame-worker, but this was only a temporary move. At 18, he joined the elite Parachute Regiment, where his natural abilities led him to progress quickly through the ranks. By the time he was 21 he had become the regiment's youngest ever platoon sergeant. Another opportunity seized.

The row across the Atlantic was already a mighty achievement but Blyth lifted his sights on something still more impressive. As the poet Lord Byron wrote to a friend in 1820, "A man must travel, and turmoil, or there is no existence." A great deal of travel and turmoil, not to mention turbulence, awaited Blyth on his next expedition, an attempt to sail alone non-stop around the world, westwards against the prevailing winds and currents. It was something that no sailor had ever tried before, but Britain has a tradition to maintain in this field.

The 20-foot open dory was duly exchanged for the 59-foot ketch *British Steel* and Blyth was underway. He set off from Southampton in October 1970, returning home to tumultuous acclaim 10 months later, mission completed. Another opportunity seized. *The Times* newspaper in London called it "the most outstanding passage ever made by one man alone". There were few serious rivals for the title Yachtsman of the Year and he added to that accolade another with his CBE from the Queen.

Though he prefers not to dwell on any particular moment when assessing his career as a yachtsman, he acknowledges the importance of that 1970-1971 expedition. "I sailed round the world against the prevailing winds single-handed non-stop; now that trip had never been attempted, let alone achieved, and generally speaking what happens after something has been done, for example to break the four-minute mile or whatever, it is being done faster or further, but it wasn't until 21 years later that somebody attempted my trip and completed it. That was a hell of an achievement, I think, to think that I was the first person to do it ever in the whole of time, it's rather like man stepping on the moon, you know you are the first to do it, that is an achievement."

That record-breaking round-the-world trip catapulted Blyth to world fame and ensured he could pursue a professional life as a yachtsman for as long as he liked. Never one to rest on his laurels, however, he followed that landmark success with a string of others. Teaming up with a crew of paratroopers in the yacht *Great Britain II* in the Round the World Race, he won the Elapsed Time Prize for the fastest yacht overall. In 1978, he won the Round Britain Race and three years later the Two-handed Transatlantic Race with Rob James. Responding to a patriotic inner voice in 1986, he co-skippered *Virgin Atlantic Challenger II* on the successful attempt to regain the Blue Riband trophy for the fastest crossing of the Atlantic.

Aside from his fine individual record, Blyth is known for making the sport of sailing more accessible to greater numbers of adventurers. He formed Challenge Business in 1989 with a view to joining together potential sponsors looking for something suitably awe-inspiring to support with adventure-seekers in search of the thrill of a lifetime. It led, notably, to the first British Steel Challenge Round-the-World Yacht Race, born from Blyth's desire to prevent the sailors with the deepest wallets and best boats winning all the biggest races. This new format involved 10 boats of identical specification, crewed by professional skippers and trained amateurs, racing along his pioneering route of 1970-1971. It evolved into the BT Global Challenge. Challenge

Business itself has evolved into a sports marketing organisation, while the official race charity Save the Children has received more than £3 million over the years.

Blyth was knighted in 1997 for services to sailing. Unable and unwilling to give it up, the silver-haired sea-dog remains as busy as ever, organising new races – the Atlantic Rowing Race, New World Challenge in America, Open 60s L'Atlantique Challenge – acquiring new businesses and passing on his love of the sport to a new generation of younger sailors. He encourages them to raise their sights and not to accept second best.

"I think many limit their horizon. They must try and go over that," he says. "They would be amazed what is achievable and can be done, and I guess one of my favourite quotes, and it's not mine, it's Field Marshal Slim's. He said that when faced with two alternatives always choose the bolder. That's the way it should be – always choose the bolder." It's something he has always done, seizing one great opportunity after the next.

"Seize the opportunity of a lifetime in the lifetime of the opportunity."

Sir Chay Blyth

Maureen Blyth waving to her husband Chay aboard British Steel II *when rounding Cape Horn during the first East/West solo circumnavigation, circa 1970.*

MEENAKSHI WADHWA

The Indian meteoriticist Meenakshi Wadhwa has always had an imaginative turn of mind.

Science gives it free expression.

"When I was eight years old, the science teacher in my school taught us that we breathe in oxygen and let out carbon dioxide," she recalls of a memorable moment in her education. "I sat there thinking: 'There must be all this carbon dioxide building up in the atmosphere. Are we going to be out of oxygen pretty soon?' I got really worried about it and ran home to my mother. 'Did you know this?' I asked. 'Is the world coming to an end?' My mother laughed and explained the cycles in nature that keep earth systems in balance. So I learned at a young age that we don't understand how much we don't understand."

Our ignorance is particularly acute in the realms of space. We understand very little about the geologic history of other planets, information that will provide a powerful insight into how our solar system and the planets and asteroids within it were formed and how they have evolved. Wadhwa's pioneering contribution to studies in this field is doing a great deal to address these lacunae in our knowledge.

Born in 1967, Wadhwa discovered an interest in rocks, minerals and natural history at a very early age. Growing up in India, however, it wasn't always clear that she would be able to forge a career in a male-dominated environment. At Punjab University colleagues put something of a dampener on her ambitions by stressing that fieldwork required an enormous amount of stamina and could be dangerous.

Such warnings did nothing to dispel Wadhwa's growing determination. She turned to the US to pursue her studies in planetary geology and geochemistry. It was an important step closer to becoming a fully fledged meteoriticist. "When I started graduate school in 1989, I discovered that my adviser – a woman – was heading off to Antarctica to be part of a team hunting for meteorites. I suddenly realised that if she could do this, so could I. Since then, as a planetary geologist who studies meteorites from Mars and the asteroids, I feel that I have gotten to explore not just remote places – like Antarctica – on earth, but also other places in our solar system." In 1994, she received her doctorate in earth and planetary sciences from Washington University.

Given our limited interaction with outer space, meteorites are an important resource for scientists to develop greater understanding of the solar system. Between 50 and 100 tons of interplanetary debris falls daily into the earth's atmosphere, of which only a tiny fraction makes it to the surface.

"From my perspective, that of a scientist studying other worlds through rocks from these faraway places, exploration means making fundamentally new discoveries about places that are challenging to reach given the current state of technology. Exploration is ultimately about gaining knowledge about the universe that surrounds us all."

Wadhwa made her debut in Antarctica in 1993 as a member of the US Antarctic Search for Meteorites Expedition. Why Antarctica? For once the answer is simple. With its barren white surface, the continent offers the ideal backdrop against which to spot these dark information capsules from space. The ice formation and movement also helps concentrate meteorites in certain regions, making their discovery that much more accessible.

Sometimes, though, you don't have to go to the end of the earth to get so lucky. Around midnight on 26 March 2003, hundreds of meteorites fell from the skies on to the Chicago suburbs of Park Forest and Olympia Fields, rather closer than Antarctica to Wadhwa's research centre at the Field Museum of Natural History in Chicago, where she is Curator of Meteoritics in the Department of Geology. Some punched holes through roofs, others damaged cars, but miraculously no one was hurt. It wasn't long before residents were hawking the meteorites to the highest bidders among dealers and collectors. Competing to get her hands on some samples, Wadhwa was delighted when the museum was able to purchase 2.7 kilograms of the 4.5 billion-year-old Park Forest meteorite for $30,000.

Such has been the young woman's impact in the rarefied world of planetary geology that in 1999 she was honoured by the International Astronomical Union which named asteroid 8356 – a Mars crossing asteroid – '8356 Wadhwa', as close to heavenly immortality as most of us will ever get. In 2005, she received a Guggenheim Fellowship which allowed her to prepare for analysing the sample of solar wind returned by the *Genesis* spacecraft in her laboratory at the Field Museum.

Some explorers argue that space exploration is lacking in romance, over-dependent on technology and by definition restricted to a scientific elite. Sir Wilfred Thesiger, for example, was profoundly pessimistic about this field of exploration. Wadhwa has a more optimistic take.

"I believe that even though there will be more and more emphasis on remote sensing and robotic exploration of our universe in the future, the human element will remain indispensable and irreplaceable. No instrument or spacecraft has yet been designed that can replace the human senses."

Wadhwa's interests inevitably overlap with those of NASA, with whom she has collaborated for some time. She has been a member of its Curation and Planning Team for Extraterrestrial Materials and the panel chief for its Cosmochemistry Program Review Panel. NASA also supported Wadhwa in the construction of a new research laboratory at the Field Museum in Chicago to analyse meteorites and other planetary materials that are likely to be brought back by future spacecraft missions.

Her ultimate hope is that her work will advance our quest for knowledge about the world that we live in way beyond the frontiers of earth's atmosphere. As Wadhwa says, only humans have the privilege of being able to learn about our origins.

"If there's one thing you learn as a scientist, it's never close your mind off to
things that seem far-fetched."

Meenakshi Wadhwa

Here with the ANSMET (Antarctic Search for Meteorites) program supported by the National Science Foundation and
National Aeronautics and Space Administration, Antarctica, 1992-1993.

JACQUES PICCARD

Some men and women aim for the heights, drawn irresistibly to scale the world's greatest mountains. Others, far fewer of them, are carried ineluctably to the depths of the ocean floor.

Jacques Piccard's family, extraordinarily, has had a taste of both extremes, though taste barely conveys the scale of its achievements. Over the past three generations the Piccards have positively devoured all challenges thrown at them by reaching hitherto impossible altitudes and depths.

In a lifetime exploring beneath the ocean waves, the Swiss scientist, engineer and explorer had his epiphany on 23 January 1960 when he and a young US Navy lieutenant called Don Walsh descended in their bathyscaphe *Trieste* to the bottom of the Marianas Trench off the coast of Guam, the deepest point on the ocean floor at 10,916 metres below the surface. The challenge of Challenger Deep, as the point is known, had been met.

The feat was comparable to Sir Edmund Hillary's achievement of reaching the summit of Everest in the sense that it took mankind into an unknown environment in which survival itself was uncertain. With seven miles of water above her *Trieste* had to withstand unfathomable pressures. The descent alone took almost five hours.

It is worth quoting at length from Piccard's account of these last fateful moments in *Seven Miles Down: The Story of the Bathyscaph Trieste*, published in 1961. Again, there are remarkable parallels to Sir Edmund Hillary's description of the famous last steps onto the summit of Everest: a sense of wonder, an awareness of the magnificence of the moment and a generous note of camaraderie.

"The bottom appeared light and clear, a waste of snuff-coloured ooze. We were landing on a nice, flat bottom of firm diatomaceous ooze. Indifferent to the nearly 200,000 tons of pressure clamped on her metal sphere, the *Trieste* balanced herself delicately on the few pounds of guide rope that lay on the bottom, making token claim, in the name of science and humanity, to the ultimate depths in all our oceans – the Challenger Deep. The depth gauge read 6,300 fathoms – 37,800 feet [subsequently revised down]. The time – 1306 hours.

"...And as we were settling this final fathom, I saw a wonderful thing. Lying on the bottom just beneath us was some type of flatfish, resembling a sole, about 1 foot long and 6 inches across. Even as I saw him, his two round eyes on top of his head spied us – a monster of steel – invading his silent realm. Eyes? Why should he have eyes? Merely to see phosphorescence? The floodlight that bathed him was the first real light ever to enter this hadal realm. Here, in an instant, was the answer that biologists had asked for decades. Could life exist in the greatest depths of the ocean? It could! And not only that, here apparently, was a true, bony teleost fish, not a primitive ray or elasmobranch. Yes, a highly evolved vertebrate, in time's arrow very close to man himself. Slowly, extremely slowly, this flatfish swam away. Moving along the bottom, partly in the ooze and partly in the water, he disappeared into his night. Slowly too – perhaps everything is slow at the bottom of the sea – Walsh and I shook hands."

Never mind once in a lifetime, that sort of discovery is once in a generation. And no one has repeated it, either. After around 20 minutes on the very bottom of the planet's surface, the pair made an ascent lasting three and a quarter hours. By the time they had returned to the surface, Piccard and Walsh had guaranteed themselves a place in exploration history. Their achievement was instantly recognised by Admiral Arleigh Burke, Chief of Naval Operations, who judged their record-breaking feat an accomplishment that "may well mark the opening of a new age in exploration of the depths of the ocean which can well be as important as exploration in space has been in the past". Marine exploration has advanced ever more rapidly after that dive showed what technology had made possible.

Piccard was born in Brussels in 1922, son of the renowned scientist and adventurer Auguste, who pioneered the pressurised cockpit that subsequently allowed balloonists to fly into the stratosphere at heights of up to 50,000 feet. Auguste turned from the heavens to the seas from the mid-1930s and Jacques grew up immersed in his father's pioneering work on underwater craft and soon became a collaborator. The *Trieste* herself was a joint effort and enabled Jacques to make many dives around Italy in the mid-1950s before she was sold to the US Navy in 1957 for the hefty price tag of $250,000. The legendary voyage with Don Walsh was *Trieste*'s 65th dive.

Piccard's interest in the marine world has not been limited to testing extremes. He is the founder of the Foundation for the Study and Protection of Seas and Lakes, based in Switzerland, and has inherited his father's passion for making exploration of the oceans more widely accessible. In the course of his career he has designed four submarines, including *Auguste Piccard*, the world's first for passengers. In 1964, during the Swiss National Exhibition, over 30,000 people were able to descend to the depths of Lake Geneva, the largest body of fresh water in western Europe.

"For me, the more people discover the sea, the greater the chance of bringing marine issues into public view and the better off we will all be."

Piccard's unique expertise has led him to work for universities, governments and even the police. Even though he was never able to recapture the excitement of the 1960 dive – how could he? – he has stuck to his interest and love with devotion. In 1986, he designed the PX44, a 40-foot, 33-ton, $4 million tourist submarine designed to take 16 passengers and a crew of two. It was considerably more comfortable than the *Trieste*.

In his later years he was delighted to have witnessed his son Bertrand maintain the family's impeccable tradition of achievement by making the first non-stop flight around the world. "I'm very, very proud of Bertrand," he says. It hardly needs saying that the pride is reciprocal.

US Navy Bathyscaphe Trieste *(1958–1963). Jacques Piccard (right),*
co-designer of the bathyscaphe, and Ernest Virgil loading iron shot
ballast into Trieste, *prior to her record 18,600 foot descent in the*
Marianas Trench, off Guam.

15 November 1959

JOHN HEMMING

The story of how John Hemming was drawn to a lifetime's involvement with the Indian tribes of Brazil is unusual, even by the standards of larger-than-life explorers. In a nutshell, it was born of tragedy.

"In 1961, I was on an expedition to survey a then unexplored area of central Brazil. After five months of cutting into forests and mapping, we were ambushed by an unknown tribe who killed my Oxford friend Richard Mason," he says. Yet he was undeterred by the grisly experience. "In the 1970s I spent almost two years visiting over 40 tribes all over Brazil, four of which were at their first contact with the outside world."

Peru and Brazil together have played a leading role in Hemming's career. For five decades he has been transfixed by Peru, visiting virtually every ruin, attracted to the most remote places and peoples in the country, setting down the fruits of his travels in a series of historical studies which have been recognised with the award of the Peruvian Order of Merit.

Hemming was born in Vancouver in 1935 because his father, who had survived the trenches of the First World War and saw the second great conflict looming, considered North America a safer bet for his son's birth. He put his pregnant wife on a cruise ship bound for Canada. Safely born, Hemming returned to England as a baby of two months.

At Eton, then at Oxford, he was a direct contemporary of Robin Hanbury-Tenison, who has become a lifetime friend. In 2003, they arrived together for the memorial service of a fellow great Old Etonian explorer, Sir Wilfred Thesiger. Though they had

pored over maps together at university and later dreamt of future expeditions in South America, they travelled together only once – across the Sahara – in the mid-1960s. In 1969, he joined Hanbury-Tenison as a co-founder of Survival International.

Hemming received public renown in 1970 with the publication of *The Conquest of the Incas*, a magisterial historical study that, according to one report, was so scholarly many believed it had been written by a famous historian using a pseudonym, rather than a 35-year-old with an undergraduate's degree. It won the 1971 Christopher Award and the Pitman Literary Award and was described by *The New York Times* as "distinguished by an extraordinary empathy, a feeling of one's way into the minds of the 16th-century Spaniards and Indians". It was also acclaimed as "the finest account of the annihilation of the Incan empire since W. H. Prescott's *History of the Conquest of Peru*", not an insignificant accolade considering the latter was published in 1847. He later got a doctorate from Oxford.

In 1975, he was appointed Director and Secretary of the Royal Geographical Society, which placed him at the heart of international exploration for the next 21 years. Aside from his contributions to literature and South American scholarship, history will judge Hemming kindly for his tremendous reinvigoration of the RGS. "During those two decades, the Royal Geographical Society was transformed in every possible way," he recalls. The number of Fellows more than doubled, the finances were reversed from the red into the black, new regional branches were opened and "lectures went from fewer than 20 half-empty events a year to packed talks every Monday". Critically, expeditions returned to centre-stage with the creation of the Expedition Advisory Centre under the inspired stewardship of Shane Winser, author of the introduction to this book. Hemming also recruited Shane's future husband Nigel to take charge of expeditions and major multidisciplinary projects were put into the field in Sarawak, Pakistan, Oman, Kenya, Tanzania, Australia, Tanzania, Nepal, Brazil and Brunei. The renewed interest in academic activities persuaded the Institute of British Geographers to return to the fold and merge with the Society.

In 1986-1987, he led a huge RGS/Brazilian expedition of 202 men and women on an ecological survey of the riverine island of Maracá, an important tropical forest reserve in Brazilian Amazonia. The expedition was also tasked to investigate forest regeneration, soils and hydrology, medical entomology and land development.

"It was the largest research effort ever organised by any European nation in Amazonia, and probably the largest ever by the RGS. It yielded several hundred species new to science, 15 books, hundreds of papers, and a lot more knowledge of the dynamics of tropical rainforests."

Hemming says of the expedition. He was awarded the Mungo Park Medal of the Royal Scottish Geographical Society in 1988, and the Gold Medal of the RGS in 1990.

Though acutely aware of the dangers faced by the world's indigenous peoples, Hemming's assessment of their future is quietly optimistic, at least in the country he knows so well.

"Indigenous peoples are extremely fit and healthy, but they are fatally vulnerable to many of our diseases, against which they have no inherited immunity. However, in the past half-century there have been improved preventive medicine and inoculation campaigns. Since the 1950s, the combined population of tribes in Brazil has quadrupled from near extinction to almost 500,000 and is rising fast. The land also supplies all their needs, from hunting, fishing and gathering, and it is the cement that keeps a tribe together, the home of their ancestors, myths and beliefs and their buffer against the colonisation frontier." Their territories were guaranteed by the 1988 constitution, he notes approvingly. Indigenous reserves in Brazil now represent 12 per cent of the country, 20 per cent of Brazilian Amazonia. They are now seen as increasingly important environmentally with the escalation in destruction of Amazon forests.

Hemming's scholarly interest in South America has continued into his seventies. In 2003, he published another highly acclaimed book, *Die If You Must: Brazilian Indians in the Twentieth Century*, the final volume in a trilogy on the history of Brazil's indigenous peoples, exploration and the clash of cultures since 1500. Writing in *Geographical* magazine, Sir Christopher Ondaatje described it as a masterpiece, "the definitive work on Brazil's indigenous peoples. It should be required reading for every red-blooded adventurer." And he should know.

Pictured at the remote Purumame waterfall on the Uraricoera River, sitting on a rock

carved by the explorers Alexander Hamilton Rice and Robert Schomurgk,

who got there in 1840 and 1925 respectively.

Maraca Rainforest Project in Northern Brazil, 1987-1988

DAVID HEMPLEMAN-ADAMS MBE OBE

For a man who says exploration and adventure are only part-time activities and declares that he is an adventurer rather than an explorer, David Hempleman-Adams has managed to notch up a remarkable number of firsts.

In 1984, he became the first person to complete a solo, unsupported expedition to the Magnetic North Pole. In 1996, he was the first Briton to walk solo and unsupported to the South Pole. In 2003, he chalked up another first, a solo balloon crossing of the Atlantic in an open wicker basket.

Undoubtedly his greatest first, however, came in 1998, when he completed what had until then been dubbed the 'impossible' grand slam of exploration. That year, after finishing the 496-mile trek to the Geographic North Pole, he became the only man in history to have reached the Geographic and Magnetic North and South Poles as well as climbing the highest peaks in all seven continents. His achievement was crowned with the award of an OBE, to add to the MBE he had been given in 1994 for services to polar exploration.

Born in 1956, he saw his parents divorce when he was nine. It was a transforming experience, not least geographically. Having had a modest childhood in a council house in Moredon – he remains fiercely loyal to nearby Swindon – he moved with his mother to a small village near Bath.

"I had been transformed from a boy from a railway town to a country lad," he writes in his autobiography *Toughing It Out.*

"I loved getting dirty, working hard, and forever being in the fresh country air. My love affair with adventure followed shortly afterwards."

Without the move, he says, his life might never have followed the same route.

At 13 he entered the Duke of Edinburgh Award Scheme and to this day credits the organisation with giving him the direction that would lead to a life of exploration and adventure. It provides, he says, "the basic building blocks of life and travel" and he remains heavily involved with the organisation today. When talking in schools, he is fond of quoting the English poet Robert Browning's words, "... a man's reach should exceed his grasp, or what's a heaven for".

Within the space of three years from entering the scheme he had won its gold award and summited a series of Welsh peaks. From that point on, Hempleman-Adams's love of mountaineering never flagged. In the mid-1980s he took a break from climbing and polar exploration to concentrate on business, specifically his epoxy resins company, Robnor. It might have proved a distraction in terms of reaching summits and poles, but financially speaking it proved time well spent. Hempleman-Adams later sold Robnorganic Systems Ltd for a considerable sum, a windfall that gave him greater freedom to pursue his interests outside the boardroom.

Having achieved everything he had set out to complete in polar and mountaineering exploration, he turned to ballooning in the new millennium. Inevitably, the new focus brought a raft of fresh firsts, albeit increasingly eccentric. In 2000, he became the first man to balloon solo to the North Pole, an expedition in the footsteps – or slipstream – of a tragically unsuccessful Swedish attempt a century earlier, described in Hempleman-Adams's touching book *At the Mercy of the Wind*.

In 2003, he made his Atlantic crossing, an 84-hour struggle against cold, sleep deprivation, hail, snow and the ear-shattering sonic boom of Concorde. A year later, he broke the world altitude record in a Roziere balloon. That year, he also received the latest in a long line of awards, the Explorer's Medal, presented to him by Buzz Aldrin at the annual Explorers Club dinner in New York. He has also been honoured by, among others, the Royal Scottish Geographical Society and the Royal Humane Society.

Hempleman-Adams says he explores "for self-fulfilment and an inner desire to travel and explore new things". Unlike some of his contemporaries, he exhibits little pretension or pomposity in delineating the compulsion that drives him. And he maintains, through this more modest approach, an admirable perspective. "Exploration and adventure are an important part of my life. However, I never get so focused on one thing that I lose sight of the real world, that is why I choose to do it part time and not as my job. The subtle difference between exploring and adventure is that I don't have to keep going out and exploring new areas. I can merely gain enjoyment from all my different adventures."

Like so many mountaineers and polar explorers, Hempleman-Adams has brushed with death in the course of his travels. Falling through an ice crevasse was one of his worst moments, an experience that still gives him nightmares. There have been others. "One moment that I truly thought I would not come out of was when I was mountaineering in the Alps with my good friend Steve Vincent some years ago," he says. "We were both young and as fit as butchers' dogs, but we got stuck in a storm and it took us 24 hours to get down off the mountain. That was the only time that we both felt like sitting down and giving up, which is something I have never experienced since. That same night in the same storm on a different mountain one of my good friends died, which really brought home how much danger we were in. In retrospect we were entirely out of our depth."

In 2004, Hempleman-Adams and co-pilot Lorne White embarked on a new challenge, flying a single-engine Cessna from Cape Columbia in northern Canada to Cape Horn, the southernmost tip of South America. Together they covered 11,000 miles in 12 days.

His most eccentric exploit came in 2005, again in a hot-air balloon, when he arranged a formal dinner with fellow explorers Bear Grylls and Alan Veal at the staggering altitude of 24,262 feet. The asparagus and salmon were said to be particularly good.

"I just think that there's adventure in all of us, and it doesn't matter if you want to climb Everest or Snowdon, but if you want to go and do it just try, that's all, just go and have a bit of fun and that's what I've done and that's what I've always tried to instil, and just push yourself."

David Hempleman-Adams

Hempleman-Adams took off from Greeley, Colorado in an attempt to break the existing altitude record of 34,943 feet. He landed in Akron, Colorado, having reached an altitude of 41,198 feet, March 2004.

ROSITA ARVIGO

There is a photograph of a couple on a trail in the jungle of Belize. On the right is a tall woman dressed in a loose pink shirt and blue trousers with a nest of curly brown hair, a pickaxe on her right shoulder and a white sack on her left. She has a dreamy, faraway expression, the look of someone who is in her element.

On the left is a much older man in simple clothes and boots, slightly stooped, carrying a sack whose strap rests across his forehead. He appears to be wearing an old baseball hat. It would be easy to conclude the woman is a botanist or jungle explorer and the man her native Indian porter.

In fact, the woman is the American ethnobotanist and natural healer Rosita Arvigo, but the old man is no porter. He is Don Elijio Panti, the late Maya shaman of Belize whose partnership and collaboration with Arvigo makes an extraordinary story.

Arvigo was born in Chicago, to immigrant parents from Iran and Italy, in 1941. After going through school and college there and following a brief marriage, she says she was drawn to the 'Flower Child' or 'Hippie Revolution' in San Francisco. She resolved to leave her "conventional life behind and follow an inner calling to experiment with new lifestyles and social paradigms, freedom of expression and ultimately a 'back-to-the-land' ethos", moving into the northern California mountains and redwood forests to join the famous Black Bear Ranch commune.

As the 1960s drew to an end, disillusioned by life in the US, Arvigo travelled south to live with a small group of friends in the Sierra Madre del Sur mountains of Mexico, where during seven years she immersed herself in the indigenous Nahuatl Indian way of life, learning Aztec healing, among many other skills. Then, one night in 1973 she had an experience which was to transform her life. A midwife asked Arvigo to help her with a problematic delivery.

"I had never seen a birth before, and didn't know what to do. The mother suddenly began haemorrhaging. The healer hurriedly sent me outside to collect roses. She made tea out of the petals and leaves which she gave the mother. Soon the haemorrhaging stopped. The healer saved the woman's life with the flowers. I knew then that was what I wanted to be – a healer who knew the secrets of the plants."

Returning to the US to live in Florida in 1976, she gravitated towards the Shangri-la Institute of Natural Hygiene and became its health director. In 1983, after a stint in Belize cultivating organic fruits for the Shangri-la health resort, she graduated with a degree in naprapathy, a form of bodywork manipulation akin to chiropractic medicine. Once again, she headed south from the States, travelling with her then husband to establish a health retreat on a 30-acre plot of uncleared jungle on the banks of the Macal River.

It was in Belize she met the enigmatic and elderly Don Elijio Panti. Since he had no assistant or apprentice working with him, his ancient healing traditions were in danger of dying with him. Enter Rosita Arvigo. Over time she befriended the old man, visiting him weekly and treating his aching back and neck with massages until, after a year, he agreed to take her on as his apprentice. She was 44 and he was 90.

For the next 12 years, Arvigo made a weekly pilgrimage to Don Elijio, trekking to his home in the Maya Mountains and staying with him for four days at a time "learning the herbs, prayers, treatments, massages, sting ray spine acupuncture and various forms of spiritual healing" from the older man. Arvigo secured the interest, collaboration and eventually sponsorship of the New York Botanical Garden, and worked in close partnership with Dr Michael Balick, one of the organisation's ethnobotanists and curators. He was at that time trying to identify tropical plants that might be used in treatments for AIDS and cancer. Arvigo set up the Belize Ethnobotany Project to record as much of the range of Belize's medicinal plants as possible. Her mission was to work closely with Don Elijio, who told her, "For every ailment or difficulty on earth, the Spirits have provided a cure – you just have to find it." Published in 1994, *Satsun: My Apprenticeship with a Maya Healer*, tells the fascinating story of their work together.

The project has grown into a database of 2,500 hundred plants of medicinal value, 500 of which Don Elijio identified before his death in 1996 at the age of 103. Arvigo's challenge was difficult enough without the added problem of land pressures and development that threatened the sanctity of the Belize jungle. In 1993, a year after she had established the Traditional Healers Foundation, the government consented to donate a 6,000-acre tract of land as the world's first medicinal plant reserve, an act that was followed by similar moves in Thailand, Mexico, Guatemala and Peru. That reserve has since been reduced to just

600 acres as commercial farming pressures continue to take their toll on the environment. Arvigo has campaigned to show that farming these medicinal plants and herbs can in fact be more lucrative than simply clearing the jungle for more crops and livestock.

Her interest in bringing herbal healing to a larger audience led her to create Rainforest Remedies in 1992, a company which directs 50 per cent of its profits towards preserving the jungles of Belize and produces a range of innovative products including Belly Be Good for upset stomachs. Her book *Rainforest Home Remedies: The Maya Way to Heal Your Body and Replenish Your Soul* was published in 2001. She has also worked with Shaman Pharmaceuticals to help find rainforest herbs to be used in anti-diabetes, anti-fungal and anti-retro-viral research.

Arvigo still maintains a private practice in Belize, the Ix Chel Wellness Centre in San Ignacio, named after the Maya goddess of medicine. When she is not there, she is likely to be on the road, globetrotting ambassador for the herbal medicine community.

Herbalist healer Rosita Arvigo holds copal, a sacred substance to the Mayans,

as she stands inside her healer's hut.

Belize, 1991

MARY ELLIS

Mary Ellis, née Wilkins, comes from a gentler age. There is no talk of sponsorship, webcams and websites, no hint of self-promotion or publicity-seeking. Among the handful of dog-eared press cuttings that document her remarkable wartime career as a pilot is one headlined "Mary was the warplane pilot", accompanied by a photograph of a slim, attractive woman standing in front of an American Mitchell bomber she had just been flying.

In reminiscing about her astonishing career in aviation she speaks in clipped tones with a matter-of-factness and modesty that come naturally to the wartime generation. Interviewing her for a local newspaper in 1994, the journalist Charlotte Hofton wrote of her admiration for Ellis and another colleague, how both women spoke without fuss of "experiences that knock much of today's feminist wittering firmly into touch". Other colleagues in the Air Transport Auxiliary (ATA) went on to write books and record television programmes but Ellis tended to avoid that sort of publicity.

She was born in 1922 in Langley Palace in the heart of Whychwood Forest, Oxfordshire, a manor house that was said to have been built by King John in 1204. She needed little time to discover a love of flying.

"My father was interested in flying and I think I must have got the genes from him. I had this wonderful feeling of wanting to fly, even when I was very small," she says. "After a memorable flight with Alan Cobham my Pa told me that if I wanted to learn to fly I could go ahead, so I did. As a schoolgirl of 16 I was not very good at hockey and was allowed to go for flying lessons at the local aero club instead. The more I flew the

more I wanted to fly, and this has remained the case all my life."

At 17 Wilkins obtained her pilot's licence. No sooner had war been declared than she heard a radio appeal for civilian pilots and promptly volunteered for the ATA – in time nicknamed the 'Ancient and Tattered Airmen and Women'. Its role was to ferry military aircraft between factories, RAF airbases and maintenance units, thus freeing up the pilots for operational duties. Its work was vital to the overall war effort, a contribution that has not received the attention it deserves in the history books.

After a successful interview and flight test Wilkins joined the ATA at Hatfield. Her intensive training course was crammed into three months, during which she learnt about navigation, meteorology, aero engines and a host of other subjects before being posted to an all-woman unit at Hamble. Once there, she never looked back. In total, she flew 75 different types of aircraft, including 400 Spitfires, and delivered almost 1,000 aircraft to 240 airfields during her time in the ATA. "I think one of the most exciting moments was the first time I flew a Wellington bomber," she says of her time in the skies, "because I had seen these big aeroplanes whilst I was learning to fly and thought it would be absolute heaven to fly one, little knowing that within a very short time I would do so."

Inevitably, being a woman in the essentially male word of wartime Britain had its unique challenges. Disbelief was not an uncommon reaction, as she recalls of one incident when she had delivered a Wellington to an RAF base. After landing, the ground crew were waiting for the pilot to emerge down a ladder from the aircraft.

"I asked if we could go to the control tower and they asked me where the pilot was. I told them I was the pilot but they didn't believe me. They went on to search the aircraft but found no one. In the end they had to believe I was the pilot."

Wilkins endured all sorts of scrapes and some tragedies in the ATA, working alongside a number of men and women who lost their lives in the war. Such was her skill she earned the nickname 'The Fog Flyer' in tribute to her ability to deliver her aircraft whatever the weather.

Another highlight of her career as a pilot, as the war ended and the ATA was disbanding, was the chance to fly the very quick, very new Meteor Jet Fighter. Wilkins was one of only three women to do so. She remembers the test pilot, who knew of her ATA experience, being very terse and unforthcoming in his briefing. "The advice he gave me was to watch the fuel gauge as they went from full to empty in 35 minutes. He also said that when coming in to land the aircraft would drop like a stone once the power was off. After looking around the cockpit and things I flew off from the factory to RAF 220 Squadron Exeter. Down there they were changing from Spitfires to Meteors and this was the

very first one they were getting. The whole squadron turned out to see it and were all somewhat amazed to see a young blonde lady climb out of their first single-seat aeroplane and I was given a tremendous reception."

In peacetime, her love of flying continued unabated. Between 1950 and 1970 she flew as a personal pilot to the owner of Sandown Airport, later becoming Britain's – and Europe's – only woman airport commandant.

Ellis would probably not recognise the word 'empower' but she is in no doubt about the importance of having a clear purpose in life.

"I think everyone should have a goal somewhere or somehow and should pursue it and try and reach the heights."

She insists, "Not to just sit there and do nothing, it's better to go on and do things to become really content." Her career as an aviation pioneer in a man's world gives ample proof of that.

Mary Ellis (née Mary Wilkins) F/o Air Transport Auxiliary.

Photographed beside a Mitchell aircraft which she was piloting.

England, 1943

BEAR GRYLLS

As a young boy growing up on the Isle of Wight and climbing with his father he had always dreamt of reaching the summit of Mount Everest. Years later, when he suffered a free-fall parachuting accident while training with the SAS in Africa, those hopes seemed to have been crushed for ever. His back was broken in three places.

"I remember lying there during those long months of recovery and suddenly this dream that I had clung to so tightly for so long, of climbing Everest, just felt a million miles away," he recalls. "It was beyond what I could believe and I remember vividly looking at the pictures my late father had given me of Everest years earlier, and taking them down. I dismissed it as something childish and something that could no longer become a reality."

Yet the picture of Everest did not recede. Instead, it spurred his recovery through months of painful rehabilitation. In 1997, Grylls became the youngest British climber to summit the Himalayan peak of Mount Ama Dablam, a mountain Sir Edmund Hillary had once described as 'unclimbable'.

A greater challenge awaited him the following year when he set his sights, at last, on Everest. He almost died after falling through a crevasse at 19,000 feet. Further difficulties came with a debilitating chest infection which held him back again at above 26,000 feet. Throughout his ordeals on the mountain he was buoyed by a Christian faith that proved remarkably resilient through repeated challenges. With the summit within striking distance, he took heart from several verses in Isaiah 40, which he had brought with him.

"Even the youths shall faint, and the young men shall utterly fail; but those who wait upon the Lord shall renew their strength; they shall mount up with wings as eagles; they shall run and not be weary; they shall walk and not grow faint."

Then, at 7.22am on 26 May 1998, three years after breaking his back and three months after beginning the ascent, Grylls made the last step of a remarkable journey and walked on to the summit of Mount Everest. In doing so he entered the *Guinness Book of Records* as the youngest Briton to have climbed the mountain and survived. He was 23. His story of the expedition, *Facing Up*, was a bestseller which propelled him on to the lucrative motivational speaking circuit.

He credits his father with inspiring a love of climbing.

"At that age though, it was as much about wanting just to be close to him, as it was about the climbing. And it was this world that I was brought up into, it was what I did, and one of the few things as a kid that I could do well. The mountains were where I found my identity, and eventually where I found intimacy."

It is the brotherhood of climbers he has always found so compelling.

"I climb because of those bonds you create with people in the extremes, and it is that which always drags me back into that dangerous world. I explore still today for one reason: through climbing, my eyes have been opened to a world of often hidden magic."

Judging by what has followed, Everest appears only to have whetted Grylls's appetite for adventure. In 2000, he led the first team to circumnavigate the UK on jetskis, raising money for the Royal National Lifeboats Institute. In 2003, he led another pioneering expedition, the first team to cross the North Atlantic Ocean in a rigid inflatable boat, raising money in the process for the Prince's Trust charity. Grylls's story of the expedition, *Facing the Frozen Ocean*, was published in 2004. A year later, he was ballooning with David Hempleman-Adams and Alan Veal, en route to breaking the world record for the highest ever open-air dinner party, slung under the balloon in formal attire at 24,262 feet.

When he is not on the lecture circuit, he can occasionally be spotted at the Travellers Club in his trademark linen suit, whatever the season. Otherwise, Grylls is likely to be on an outlandish expedition out in the wilds. In 2005, the year he was awarded an honorary commission in the Royal Navy as a lieutenant-commander, he was paramotoring over remote jungle plateaux in Venezuela in an attempt to reach Auyán Tepuy, the towering sandstone cliffs made famous by Sir Arthur Conran Doyle's 1912 novel *The Lost World*.

"I was in a South American jungle amongst high rainforest plateaux that are totally unmapped and untouched by human footfall," he says. 'The map simply said: 'no data available'. And this produces in me an excitement, a quickening of the pulse, a longing to see what no one has seen, and it is this, that is to me, exploration."

Unlike so many of his fellow explorers, Grylls says his greatest moments have not been out in the field so much as returning from them. "The honest answer is that often it is that sweet moment of coming home! After so much has happened 'out there', whether it is the good stuff, like the summits, or whether it is the bad, like the tragic loss of someone's life, I find I crave familiarity, safety, comfort and home. And it is often these things that drive me on."

A constant companion on his high-spirited wanderings is his father's weathered little New Testament, and a simple quote inside that says: "Never will I leave you, nor will I forsake you."

Another favourite motivator is the regimental poem of the SAS (see opposite).

"We are the Pilgrims, master; we shall go
Always a little further: it may be.
Beyond the last blue mountain barred with snow,
Across that angry or that glimmering sea."

Crevasse crossing in the Western Cwm, often called the Valley of Silence *on Everest,
at 20,000 feet, May 1998.*

JEAN-MICHEL COUSTEAU

The great oceans of our planet have one 'first family' to thank for efforts to preserve them. Jacques Cousteau was the pioneering explorer who opened the underwater world to ordinary men and women by perfecting the aqualung, a cylinder of compressed air attached to a diver's mouth through a pressure-regulating valve. It enabled divers to stay underwater for hours at a time.

Jacques' son, Jean-Michel, has taken his father's passion for the sea several steps further. If the world's oceans could elect a single ambassador to represent their interests in the modern era of environmental pollution and climate change, there can be little doubt they would choose Jean-Michel. Such is the man's involvement with the seas and the times in which he has been immersed in them, it's almost a surprise to find he doesn't have a set of gills, a fin and a tail.

He sees himself as a discoverer and an adventurer who always likes to see "what is on the other side of the hill", but he is nurtured by more than natural curiosity.

"I think I have a profound sense of responsibility because I know how privileged I am and all I want to do is share what I have found. Now perhaps more than before, we find out that there is a lot happening to our planet that most people do not know is happening."

"There is a critical opportunity to convey to as many people as possible the sense of adventure, discovery, and our responsibility to tiptoe on the planet. We are using the ocean as a garbage can, a universal sewer and at the same time it is a life-support system that we need to survive."

Born in Toulon in 1938, his first contact with the sea came as a seven-year-old when he was "thrown overboard" by his father wearing newly-invented scuba gear. It was the first of many exploratory dives from his father's famous boat *Calypso*. As a child he started dreaming of building new Atlantises – underwater cities – and pursued studies in architecture to help realise that dream. He graduated from the Paris School of Architecture in 1964 and jokes today that he is still waiting for his first client.

His father, who died in 1997, asked Jean-Michel to "carry forward the flame of his faith", something he has done to a greater degree than Jacques could ever have hoped for. In 1999, he founded Ocean Futures Society, a marine conservation and education organisation. Its motto is, 'Protect the ocean, and you protect yourself.' Cousteau knows he has his work cut out to reverse the damage mankind has already caused.

"All my and all my team's mission is affected by the sense of urgency and to let the people know about what's going on, ultimately by making people understand and change our habits. One day my dad told me – it was very powerful in a sense, even though it was very few words – 'People protect what they love.' So that's why I explore and what motivates me."

Apart from what he sees as his curiosity and sense of moral responsibility, Cousteau considers exploration as personally restorative. "When things go really bad, like when I lost my dad, the first thing I did was to go diving so there is a certain serenity underwater, a calm and almost religious environment which makes you so peaceful and so at peace with yourself and it also clarifies things. It eliminates the details of life and points out what is important and what is not."

Following his father's example, he has brought the oceans on to our screens, producing over 70 films, many of them award-winning. As a reviewer said of one of his latest, *Sharks 3D*, "Jean-Michel Costeau's tribute to the shark gets so up close and personal, you'd swear you could scrape the moss off the marine predator's teeth." It reminded viewers, too, that only 68 of around 400 shark species are dangerous. Together they account for 12 deaths a year, while humans, who have long dramatised the animal's awesome killing potential, reportedly slaughter 100 million to 200 million a year.

In 2002, his enormous contribution was recognised when he became the first person to represent the environment at the opening ceremony of the Olympics in 2002. He has received numerous other awards, including the inaugural Ocean Hero Award from the international advocacy organisation Oceana in 2003. Andrew Sharpless, its chief executive, said of him: "The extraordinary spirit of the Cousteau family is alive and well in the work of Jean-Michel. Jean-Michel has inherited the mantle of ocean explorer and caretaker of the seas from his father, and he has swum with it. His work has inspired a love of the seas in people all over the world, and I can't think of a more deserving recipient."

Though he is interested in the future of space exploration, Cousteau sees the study and preservation of our more immediate environment – particularly the seas – as more pressing.

"We know more about Mars than we do about the bottom of the ocean. We really need to focus on our life-support system. If we don't do that, if we don't focus on exploring the ocean and understanding the importance of the ocean, we have much to lose."

"The ocean is potentially a formidable resource, not just of minerals but compounds which can be mimicked by the pharmaceutical industry to create drugs to take care of some of our diseases. We will continue to eliminate species by our carelessness and degrade our environment if we do not change our ways," he says.

Through his position as president of Ocean Futures Society, he remains an indefatigable advocate and ambassador for the sea, globetrotting to raise awareness among policy-makers, lobbying world leaders and continuing his mission to educate the next generation of men and women who will carry forward the flame once more. "I think that if we can make more young people understand it and really enjoy it, they will protect it because they will love it," he says.

"I am a discoverer, an adventurer, I like to see what is on the other side of the hill so my curiosity is really what dictates why I need to go out there. At the same time I think I have a profound sense of responsibility because I know how privileged I am and thus all I want to do is share what I have found."

Jean-Michel Cousteau

Jean-Michel Cousteau finds a pod of killer whales off the Vestmannaeyjar Archipelago, Iceland, 1999.

Sir RANULPH FIENNES

Sir Ranulph Twisleton-Wykeham Fiennes is an aristocratic adventurer of the old school, a tight-lipped Old Etonian, former SAS officer and descendant of Charlemagne.

The motto of his family, which traces its roots back to the ninth century, is 'Look for a brave spirit', an appropriate tag for a man who has fought in the Dhofar campaign, wandered through deserts, trekked to the poles and circumnavigated the globe. *The Guinness Book of Records* calls Fiennes, who is generally known as Ran, 'The World's Greatest Living Explorer'. His mother's verdict is less high-flown. "I always worried he would turn out very mad or bad," she once said. "Thank goodness he turned out mad."

When Fiennes was born in Windsor in 1944, he had already lost his father months earlier, a colonel in the Royal Scots Greys, killed in the Second World War. His early years were spent in South Africa, his grandmother's homeland, where his time at school taught him he was better at fighting than academic work. After returning to prep school in Britain he scraped into Eton, where a poor academic record prevented him from moving on to Sandhurst and a career as a regular officer in his father's footsteps. He took a fairly dim view of the skills he learned during short commissions in uniform. "I spent eight years in the army, after which the only thing I knew how to do was lead three 70-ton tanks in withdrawal, which doesn't exactly look good on a CV," he observed with his usual dry humour.

His time in the services included a stint in the SAS, from which he was summarily dismissed for deliberately blowing up a Twentieth Century-Fox film set in the idyllic English village of Castle Coombe, Wiltshire, professedly on environmental grounds but more probably because he was fond of high jinks. 'Bomber Baronet Captured in Prettiest Village', the headlines announced. His mother fainted in shock. From 1968-1970, he was a captain in the Sultan of Oman's armed forces, where he won a medal for his part in the Dhofar campaign.

With his military career over and nothing forthcoming in the City, Fiennes turned to exploration. His first expedition, in the steps of Victorian explorers, was a hovercraft journey up the White Nile. Higher profile was the first circumnavigation of the earth along the polar axis, which required almost three years of non-stop travel over 52,000 miles between 1979 and 1982. His wife Ginny, whom he married in 1970 (they first met when he was 12 and she nine), accompanied Fiennes on his expeditions until the mid-1980s, when she returned to a quieter life farming in Somerset and grew used to not seeing him. Asked once what was the key to their successful relationship, she replied, "Probably because he's away all the time."

Following an unexpected phone call from Armand Hammer, the octogenarian millionaire and chairman of Occidental Petroleum, Fiennes donned a suit and tie for the next eight years and became a consultant. But he was not at home in the corporate world and a return to the expedition world was inevitable.

Like so many explorers before him, Fiennes was drawn irresistibly to the poles. In 1990, he achieved the world record for unsupported northerly travel. In 1991, after eight expeditions and 24 years of trying, he discovered the fabulously rich lost city of Ubar in southern Oman, T. E. Lawrence's 'Atlantis of the Sands', the legendary ancient trading centre of Arabia referred to in the Koran and *Arabian Nights*, which had disappeared into the desert and had haunted generations of treasure-seekers and explorers. He described this as his greatest expedition achievement, qualifying the success with the wry – some would call it perverse – acknowledgement: "You know, in a way, having found it was a bit disappointing because, then, you couldn't go on looking for it."

Interviewers invariably describe him as unforthcoming and impenetrable. Countless journalists have been fobbed off with the pithy reply "Because it's my job" when asking why he stretched himself to such limits. Catching him in a more loquacious mood, another was told,

"I go on expeditions for the same reason an estate agent sells houses – to pay the bills."

Describing his conversation with Fiennes for the BBC radio programme 'In the Psychiatrist's Chair', Anthony Clare said it was like "stirring a void with a teaspoon". Those who know him better see him as a single-minded loner, courageous but kind. Recalling that particular conversation, Fiennes was characteristically defiant, judging it in military terms rather than as an interview. "I found it quite satisfactory that he had spent 45 minutes trying to get to the bottom of me, how I tick, and hadn't succeeded. I found that a victory. I spent a lot of time with the special forces learning how to resist interrogation. I took it on as a project."

Over the years his expeditions have raised millions of pounds for medical research and in 1993 he was awarded an OBE for 'human endeavour and charitable services'. He has been serially awarded by, among other organisations, the Royal Geographical Society, which gave him the illustrious Founder's Medal, the Royal Institute of Navigation and the Explorers Club of New York. In 1984 he was presented with the Polar Medal with Bar by the Queen.

Though he spoke sometimes about opting for a more sedentary life after fifty, he was unable to shake off the expedition bug. In 2000, he attempted to become the first person to walk alone and unsupported to the North Pole. Only a week into the journey, he was forced to abort after developing severe frostbite in his left hand. He later had the tops of his fingers amputated. In 2003, he suffered a heart attack but, never one to allow small details like that to interfere in his life, celebrated his recovery later that year by running seven marathons in seven days on seven continents.

"My admiration for Ran is unbounded and thank God he exists.
The world would be a far duller place without him."

Prince Charles

Ranulph Fiennes manhauling a sledge, North Pole unsupported expedition, 1990.

HEINRICH HARRER

There are some mountaineers who seem to court drama with the intensity of a Hollywood starlet smouldering in front of the camera. None more so than Heinrich Harrer, the Austrian climber whose life reads like a **Boy's Own** *adventure.*

Born in Hüttenberg in 1912, he studied geography and sports at the Karl Franzen University in Graz and competed as a skier in Hitler's infamous Berlin Olympics of 1936. He subsequently came to notice in 1938 as a member of the mountaineering team that made the remarkable first ascent of the near-vertical North Face – or 'Murder Wall' – of the Eiger, a climb later celebrated in his 1958 book *The White Spider*, named after the ice field that tops the rocky face. Having joined the SS, his fortunes took a profound turn for the worse a year after his triumph on the Eiger when, with the outbreak of war, he was arrested by the British during an abortive climbing expedition on the then unclimbed peak of Nanga Parbat in India.

Cue another epic physical achievement. In 1944, after two unsuccessful bids, he made a dramatic escape into the mountains disguised as an Indian workman with his colleague Peter Aufschnaiter, the two POWs finally arriving in the forbidden city of Lhasa after a 20-month marathon on foot in which they had crossed 65 passes, struggling over 1,000 miles of terrain above 16,000 feet. In the Tibetan capital he befriended the young Dalai Lama and, having fallen in love with this mountain-locked kingdom and resolved to stay, became the younger man's tutor. He taught him English, geography, maths and science, even dabbling in cinema by rigging up a dilapidated projector to screen the film of Laurence Olivier's *Henry V* to a room of bemused abbots who were scandalised by the love scenes.

He made himself useful as a salaried official of the Tibetan government by translating foreign news and taking up a position as court photographer. Living as a minor noble in the city, Harrer enjoyed unprecedented access to the Tibetan nobility and witnessed their exotic ceremonies and rituals first-hand, a privileged position that allowed him to record the life of an entire society and the romantic, unforgiving landscape in which it lived, lovingly captured in a magnificent collection of photography. He says, looking back on his life,

"I grew up in the mountains and soon realised, if you don't leave your village, you can never experience adventure. And if you don't leave behind the shores of your continent, you can never encounter a great adventure."

His greatest adventure ended with the invasion of the Chinese army at the end of 1950.

Their arrival betokened his reluctant departure in the spring of 1951. Published in 1954, *Seven Years in Tibet*, the fabulous story of his time in the country, was one of the most successful travel books of all time. Translated into 53 languages, it sold more than four million copies and in 1997 was belatedly made into a $70 million blockbuster film with Brad Pitt as the young Harrer.

In his most famous book he admitted he would always feel home-sick for Tibet. It was the happiest time of his life. "I often think I can still hear the cries of wild geese and cranes and the beating of their wings as they fly over Lhasa in the clear cold moonlight," he wrote. "My heartfelt wish is that my story may create some un-derstanding for a people whose will to live in peace and freedom has won so little sympathy from an indifferent world."

Though his explorations continued and he went on to write another 22 books, Tibet remained his abiding love. In the face of Chinese aggression against the country, he was a single-minded and passionate champion for human rights there, his involve-ment in the struggle rooted in an enduring friendship with the Dalai Lama, who fled to India in 1959.

He returned to Tibet four decades after his first visit and was upset by the environmental damage the Chinese had caused. In 2002, the Tibetan spiritual leader, with whom he shared the same birthday, attended Harrer's ninetieth birthday celebrations and presented him with the Light of Truth Award for his unswerving support of Tibetan rights.

In 1997, with the release of the Brad Pitt movie, Harrer came under attack for his Nazi past, an unwelcome discovery un-earthed by an Austrian radio journalist delving in German archives in Berlin. The controversy intensified with the publica-tion of a photograph showing Harrer standing next to Hitler, who was personally congratulating him and the other members of the successful Eiger team at a sports rally in Breslau. Challenged to explain his membership, however brief, of the SS,

Harrer responded: "Well, I was young. I was, I admit it, extremely ambitious and I was asked if I would become the teacher of the SS at skiing. I have to say I jumped at the chance. I also have to say that if the Communist Party had invited me I would have joined. And if the very Devil had invited me I would have gone with the Devil."

He also stressed his absence from Austria between 1939-1952, said he had worn the SS uniform only once (at his first wedding in 1938) and reiterated his repugnance of the Hitler government and everything it stood for. It was an explanation accepted by Simon Wiesenthal, scourge of Nazi war criminals, but the whole experience left a sour taste in the mouth.

Exploration, above all life in the mountains, gave Harrer his greatest pleasure. He was asked once by the Dalai Lama what he loved about climbing mountains. He replied,

"The absolute simplicity, that's what I love. When you're climbing your mind is clear and free from all confusions. You have focus. And suddenly the light becomes sharper, the sounds are richer and you're filled with the deep, powerful presence of life."

Heinrich Harrer died on 7 January 2006 at the age of 93.

"*Wherever I live, I shall feel homesick for Tibet. I often think I can still hear the cries of wild geese and cranes and the beating of their wings as they fly over Lhasa in the clear cold moonlight. My heartfelt wish is that my story may create some understanding for a people whose will to live in peace and freedom has won so little sympathy from an indifferent world.*"

From Seven Years in Tibet *by Heinrich Harrer*

Heinrich Harrer with a young monk on the roof of the Deprung Monastery, Tibet, circa 1940.

Dr JERRI NIELSEN

There are adventures at the South Pole and then there are the experiences of Dr Jerri Nielsen.
Her remarkable story of a winter at the Amundsen-Scott research station, where she discovered she had
a highly aggressive form of breast cancer with no possible rescue available for months, was so filled with
drama and pathos it was turned into a film – Ice Bound – with Susan Sarandon in the lead role.

Published in 2001, Nielsen's book *Ice Bound: A Doctor's Incredible Battle for Survival at the South Pole* was an instant and inevitable bestseller. It took its place, said *The New York Times*, "among the great Antarctic adventure stories".

For those Wwho knew her it was no surprise that Nielsen should find her way to the pole in 1999. She had long enjoyed a roving spirit. "I began to dream as a young girl riding my bicycle," she says of this early instinct to explore. "A bike gives you total solitude and yet places one directly in the environment. With wind in my hair and my heart pumping, I was able to imagine myself greater than I was and anywhere I wished to be."

After a turbulent divorce in her mid-forties, the place she wished to be most – after spotting the irresistible magazine advert "Wanted: Doctors for polar medicine" – was the South Pole. She booked herself a position as the sole doctor at the station, enlisting for a year's work at the end of the earth. When the last plane left in March, there was no prospect of another aircraft landing for eight or nine months. With Antarctic winter temperatures averaging minus 78 degrees Celsius and darkness lasting six months, flying conditions are as inhospitable as anywhere on the planet. It doesn't matter how ill you are. An airlift is out of the question.

Yet within weeks of that plane leaving, Nielsen discovered a lump above her right breast. At this point she preferred to keep the horrifying discovery private. Her first reaction was instructive. Putting her colleagues first, who although they did not know it were suddenly in the unenviable position of losing their doctor, Nielsen started organising the medical facility "so that people when I died or got really sick" would know where to find everything, properly labelled with accompanying instructions.

By June, the mass had grown and she knew cancer was the most likely diagnosis. She went public with the revelation. Then, in an extremely dangerous mission, medicine and medical equipment were dropped by air. To confirm whether she had cancer, Nielsen had to perform the first of two biopsies on herself, having trained a welder to help in the process by practising on a potato and a chicken. After inserting a needle into her breast to extract fluid, the samples were placed on a slide and, with great difficulty, stained in order to facilitate diagnosis. Then, in an inspired piece of Heath-Robinson wizardry, her girlfriend Lisa hooked up a microscope, camera and computer and used the Internet to transmit pictures of the biopsy samples back to the US. These days that might appear routine business. Six years ago, doing that sort of thing from the South Pole with limited equipment was nothing less than a life-saving act of brilliance.

The diagnosis from Dr Kathy Miller, 11,600 miles away in the Indiana University Cancer Center, was globular carcinoma of the breast, stage II C. In three words, severe breast cancer. Nielsen's chances of survival looked slim. "I was certain I was going to die at the South Pole," she says. "I'm still shocked I didn't."

What followed next was a triumph of teamwork, a story of fellowship in adversity. With Nielsen supervising her colleagues, she started chemotherapy, communicating with Dr Miller by email. The chemo regimen she was given was designed to be effective without inducing the sort of side-effects that would prevent her working as the station's doctor. Without a pump, Nielsen was forced to rely on her welder colleague to time the IVs with his watch, drip by solitary drip.

But the treatments struggled to combat the growing tumour and in October, six months after detecting the lump, Nielsen was going to die if she was not removed from the station. At last, only two weeks early, the 109th National Guard landed and airlifted her to New Zealand, thence to the US for treatment.

Having endured all the pain and hardship of breast cancer at the South Pole, there was little respite on returning to the US. In fact, Nielsen's travails continued. She underwent a lumpectomy, took more drugs for 12 weeks, endured a further eight weeks of radiation and then, after a severe infection which almost killed her, a mastectomy.

These life-changing experiences at the ole would have broken many weaker people. For Nielsen, however, they were a cathartic event, an encounter that helped her achieve spiritual solace. She insists,

"You have to live life completely. I believe that the need to explore is internal. Someday, geneticists will map that place in one's DNA that forces some people to the heights and depths of experience, while permitting others greater comfort in the lack of change."

Nielsen's near-death experience in the most extreme environment on earth – drop a wet towel and it freezes to the floor – put her own life into a broader perspective. "I learned that all these little things that we worry about are meaningless," she says. "Totally meaningless. It's ridiculous. So it's nice to, at age 50, like me, have already faced death. Now I know that I shouldn't be afraid of it. So I can do anything that's dangerous because, what the heck, right?"

For as long as mankind inhabits planet earth, there will be no end to exploration because, Nielsen argues, "There is no end to what man can imagine. The more we know and create, the greater and more extreme our exploration will be. When we had ships, we imagined sailing around the earth. Now we have spacecraft."

Wherever we go, we will forever be detecting new frontiers – and then crossing them.

"People who always succeed really have a collection of failures. It's only when you truly run up against something that you can look back and say, 'I did it. I really lived'."

Dr Jerri Nielsen

Jerri Nielsen standing at the Amundsen-Scott Base, 1 January 1999.

Sir WILFRED THESIGER

Born in 1910 into an aristocratic family in what was then Abyssinia, the man who one day would become the world's greatest living explorer had the sort of exotic African upbringing his fellow English schoolboys could only dream of.

At the age of six, Wilfred Thesiger watched, awe-struck, as the victorious armies of Ras Tafari, later Emperor Haile Selassie, marched into Addis Ababa, where Thesiger's father was British Minister, parading their prisoners in chains. It was a defining moment. "I believe that day implanted in me a life-long craving for barbaric splendour, for savagery, colour and the throb of drums," he later wrote.

Thesiger's was that most conventional of upper-class English educations. After prep school, he moved to Eton, for which he retained a life-long affection and, in 1928, to Oxford University, where he captained the boxing team. The desire for adventure still burnt unquenched and he wasted little time in hunting out his barbaric splendour. On going down from Oxford, he led an expedition across Abyssinia to chart the source of the Awash River in 1933. Travelling through the country of the murderous Danakil, a tribe for whom killing and castration were marks of manhood, Thesiger and his party were fortunate to survive. Against all the odds, the young man's pioneering expedition was a success.

A career in the Sudan Political Service was a natural progression in 1934, but like Sir Richard Burton before him, Thesiger's interests lay in exploration and adventure, not the humdrum administration of empire. In Darfur he quickly mastered the art of riding a camel, hard and fast. "I was exhilarated by the sense of space, the silence, and the crisp clearness of the sand," he later wrote.

"I felt in harmony with the past, travelling as men had travelled for untold generations across the deserts, dependent for their survival on the endurance of their camels and their own inherited skills."

It helped define his credo, "the harder the life, the finer the person".

Thesiger always insisted it was the people and not the places that stimulated his desire to explore. In 1941, longing for action, he volunteered to join David Stirling's fledgling Special Air Service and fought behind enemy lines in the Western Desert with great distinction, winning the DSO. In the latter half of the 1940s, he turned his attention to one of the few remaining blank spaces on the world atlas: the Rub al Khali, or Empty Quarter, of the Arabian peninsula.

For five years he lived with the Bedu and twice crossed the Empty Quarter by camel, also working discreetly for British intelligence in the guise of a locust eradication official.

Had it not been for his mother and some publishing friends who persuaded him to write about his journeys, there would have been no *Arabian Sands*. Published in 1959, it conferred instant fame and status as a serious explorer. Eight years living in southern Iraq during the 1950s led to the publication of *The Marsh Arabs*, which many regard, with *Arabian Sands,* as his finest work, extolling a way of life that has since been hounded into extinction.

Though he never intended to write, he discovered in himself a highly evocative style of sparse and simple prose, accompanied by his own exquisite photography. Thesiger's greatest legacy may be his superb photographic record, a portrait of ancient cultures around the world, many of which no longer exist. He donated his collection of 25,000 negatives to the Pitt-Rivers Museum in Oxford.

As the twentieth century accelerated before him like a great tidal wave, swamping all before it, ending the mystery of the unknown and threatening the tribal peoples that inhabited it, Thesiger made further journeys to far-flung parts: to Persia, Iraqi Kurdistan, Pakistan, Afghanistan and Yemen, collected in *Desert, Marsh and Mountain.* The relentless desire to explore and his abiding dislike of the contemporary world was fleshed out in his 1987 autobiography *The Life of My Choice.*

Thesiger understood the paradox inherent in his wilderness journeys, that his travels in unexplored Arabia played their part in modernising an ancient civilisation. "I realise that the maps I made helped others, with more material aims, to visit and corrupt a people whose spirit once lit the desert like a flame," he wrote.

It was to Africa that Thesiger returned to live out his last days with the Samburu tribe of northern Kenya. With his funds fast diminishing as a result of his generosity to the tribesmen, he returned to England in 1997. Thesiger never married – it would have been a "crippling handicap" he once said – and his last years were lonely.

He was still writing in his nineties and remained a beacon for a younger generation of travel writers and explorers. They regularly made the pilgrimage to his retirement home in suburban Surrey to talk to the man with the most remarkable face they had ever seen, whose manners and conversation owed more to Edwardian England than to the contemporary life he deplored.

The great explorer had lost his bearings in the modern world, though he remained the favourite son of the Royal Geographical Society and the Travellers Club. The internal combustion engine was one of the most monumental disasters to befall mankind, he would often say, a veritable 'abomination' (never mind that he had always hopped on and off planes as he liked, one of the many benefits of a private income). Disregarding the excitement of space travel, he would pronounce that exploration had no future. Deeply courteous, impeccably dressed, marooned in the twenty-first century, he was surrounded by bookshelves bearing Burton, Lawrence, Conrad and Kipling. It frustrated him that his failing eyesight meant he could barely read them.

Nothing ever compared to his years in the desert, he would tell his visitors sadly.

"I knew that I had made my last journey in the Empty Quarter and that a phase in my life was ended," he wrote in Arabian Sands. "Here in the desert I had found all that I asked; I knew that I should never find it again."

Sir Wilfred Thesiger died on 24 August 2003. His memorial service at Eton Chapel was a gathering of the great and the good of British exploration. Movingly, there was a message of support from the Marsh Arabs of Iraq, in which they expressed their sympathy for Britain's great loss.

"*It is not the goal but the way there that matters, and the harder the way the more worthwhile the journey.*"

Sir Wilfred Thesiger

Thesiger's party in the Empty Quarter, 1948.

CHRISTINA DODWELL

It is not often you feel grateful to thieves. Yet when she looks back on her career, the inveterate traveller Christina Dodwell probably doesn't have too many hard feelings towards the two men she was travelling with across Africa.

Certainly, they would not score highly in the gentlemanly behaviour stakes. In the middle of the night, they abandoned Dodwell and her other female companion and took the Land Rover – containing food and maps – with them for good measure. Had they not done so, Dodwell might never have embarked on a life of exploration on either two legs or four.

Many, if not most, 24-year-olds would have been sufficiently daunted to throw in the towel. Instead, Dodwell was galvanised, her spirit of adventure unleashed. The journey continued, first with her companion, later alone, metamorphosing into a three-year, 30,000-mile footloose odyssey across Africa. She walked and rode – camels, horses, zebras – and even resorted to a dugout canoe, overcoming tick-bite fever, aggressive jackals and a diet of fresh blood and yoghurt along the way. *Travels with Fortune: An African Adventure*, the story of the journey and the first of Dodwell's nine books, was published to widespread acclaim in 1979.

Light-fingered cads aside, Dodwell's childhood had prepared her well for a life on the move. Born in Nigeria in 1951, she had a suitably exotic upbringing which she says helped her get started in exploration. "I'd always had longings to be elsewhere and I was born and raised in West Africa so that I didn't necessarily think the same as everybody else when I was at school.

My mother always said that it was all right to be different – if you are different that's OK – and that gave me the freedom to follow my own path. I didn't have to be like everybody because I'd been born and raised in the bush."

Her first African journey, as is so often the case, whetted her appetite for more. It also confirmed her preference for the freedom of travelling on four legs rather than the more self-enclosed world of travelling by four wheels.

"I learnt the difference; when you have a vehicle you are actually wonderfully self-contained and don't need very much of anyone, you have water, food, all your sort of breakdown gear, you need very little. What I love when I travel with a horse is that I need everything, to find water, to find village markets. I have endless needs, from helping with the horse's feet to this and that, which brings one continually into contact with people."

In 1980, she set off for what turned into a two-year journey to reach and cross Papua New Guinea, alternating again between two legs and four – she gave her New Guinea mount the studiously unromantic name Horse – not to mention four months in a canoe making the first navigation of the Sepik River. This was also a journey of linguistic discovery, an encounter with Pidgin and memorable expressions such as "Hoss brok-im leg. Im bugarap tru," translated as "The horse has broken his leg. He is well and truly buggered." To which she replied cheerfully, "Im orait, im lusim skin ta'sol," meaning, "He's all right, he's only grazed his skin."

Papua New Guinea attracted Dodwell because it was remote and largely uncharted. She has had a long love affair with mountains and says she is always drawn to those places that are most inaccessible. "Exploration means the freedom to go where the mountains look best, where you can see the pass, where you can feel your way. When you are up in the mountains and you can work out your route for the rest of the day – I could go over that saddle there and perhaps along that valley, if I do that it may lead me to the rather funny-shaped hill with the cliff that I can see in the far distance and it's got some sort of a something on top. It's the freedom from roads, from vehicles... I enjoy the fun of not knowing, about that wonderful blank emptiness of the future which is just waiting to be filled."

After Africa and Papua New Guinea, Dodwell's exploration – and more often than not riding – bug continued undiminished with journeys to Turkey, Iran, Greece, Siberia, China and Madagascar. She flew by microlight across West Africa and discovered a dinosaur skeleton in the Sahara in the process. Why does she explore? Her answer is quintessentially straightforward. "Because nobody stops me, because it's OK, perhaps it's because I have an awful curiosity – this is the main reason – I just want to find out what it's like there, what it's like being there and being part of that other world – and curiosity, whether it be what's round the next bend in the river or what's over the other side of the world.

"Sometimes when I am now working in Madagascar my eyes will fall on a bit of map, and I will think,

'Ooh there doesn't seem to be anything in there' – I love seeing the remote and unknown places – I want to go where nobody has felt there was anything of any importance, I want to go to the blank bits of the map and see for myself."

In 1989, Dodwell was awarded the Mungo Park Medal by the Royal Scottish Geographical Society. Two year later, she married and now lives on a farm in Monmouthshire, that is when she is not working and broadcasting in Africa. Much admired by her contemporaries, in Sir Chris Bonington's words, "Christina Dodwell continues the tradition of many renowned travellers, of Gertrude Bell, Annie Taylor, Isabella Bird, Freya Stark and Ella Maillart."

She is also motivated to get actively involved with the places that have made the most impression on her. Dodwell's experience of Madagascar and her desire to help alleviate its hardship led to the foundation of The Dodwell Trust in 1995, a charity dedicated to community development and family health.

Her advice to anyone considering a life in exploration is uncompromising and simple.

"Don't hesitate, if you stand there and worry about it forever you are not going to go. The best is to set off and do your best as you go along."

Christina riding north on the shore of Lake Turkana, during her 1,000 kilometres horseback journey through Kenya and Ethiopia.

Africa, 1979

TIM SEVERIN

In an era when a good deal of exploration is little more than glorified adventure, Tim Severin represents the patience and discipline of a more rigorous generation. His expeditions across the world's oceans may have been thrilling, but in no sense were they thrill-seeking. Severin has always had greater ambition than that.

He says he has two clear criteria when considering whether to go ahead with a project. "First, it must be original, something that no one has ever done before – in modern times, that is. Second, it must stand a reasonable chance of advancing knowledge." Originality does not seem to have been a problem, when you look at the range of his missions to advance our understanding of past ages.

It was the watchword of the 1976-1977 'Brendan' expedition, his attempt to prove a sixth-century Irish monk and missionary might have made a journey to the New World as recorded in a ninth-century Latin text *Navigatio Sancti Brendani Abbatis*, the *Voyage of St Brendan the Abbot*. How to demonstrate it? Straightforward.

> *"For me, exploration means problem solving: that is, putting a theory to a practical test and trying to puzzle out the solution by practical experiment. Thus, problem: could Irish monks have crossed the North Atlantic in leather boats a thousand years before Columbus? Method and test: build a leather boat with early medieval materials and make a voyage to test the possibility."*

He did exactly that, taking two years to construct a replica leather boat, and then sailed the vessel 4,500 miles from Ireland to Newfoundland via the Hebrides, the Faroe Islands and Iceland. The death-defying journey threw up the fascinating possibility that Brendan and his brethren might have discovered the New World almost one thousand years before Columbus. Published in 1978, *The Brendan Voyage: An Epic Crossing of the Atlantic by Leather Boat* was a runaway success all over the world. Most writers would be delighted to see their book translated into a single foreign language. Severin's was translated into 27.

Born in 1940 in Assam, India, where his father was a tea planter, Severin says his desire to explore stemmed from his early exposure to other cultures. An English boarding school from the age of six imbued the prerequisite quality of independence. After leaving Tonbridge, he went on to read geography at Oxford University, where he specialised in medieval Asian exploration, the perfect springboard for his debut 'Marco Polo Expedition', he recalls with characteristic self-effacement.

"In the second long vacation as an Oxford undergraduate two companions and I set out to follow the route of Marco Polo on very unsuitable motorcycles. The trip was a success, at least in the fact that we got back in reasonable shape and a publisher asked me to write a book about my experience. From that moment forward, I wondered if I could make a living by making similar trips and writing about them."

Tracking Marco Polo, published when he was still only 24, was his first stab at it and showed that he probably could. A steady stream of highly acclaimed books and films has flowed ever since.

No sooner had he returned from the epic Brendan expedition than Severin set his sights on assessing the Sindbad story. Back to ship construction again, this time a medieval vessel capable of sailing the 6,000-mile trade route popularised in *The Arabian Nights*. This time it was a 90-foot craft made from 140 tons of hardwood, propelled along by 2,900 square feet of sail. This expedition, like all his others, was characterised by minute attention to detail. The hardwood was specially selected in India; 50,000 coconut husks were used to make 400 miles of coconut rope to bind the wooden ribs and planks together. Eventually, the *Sohar*, named after the supposed home of Sindbad in Oman, was launched in late 1980 and Severin and crew set sail from Dubai to China.

After enduring the miseries and triumphs common to sailors of another era – think rats, cockroaches, days of boredom, dwindling food and water supplies – they made it. Severin remembers it as one of the many highlights of his watery career, "sailing up the Pearl River in a medieval Arab ship at the conclusion of 'The Sindbad Voyage', with a superb and jubilant crew of Arabs and Westerners."

There was no letting up after Marco Polo, Brendan and Sindbad. Other historical legends to face the Severin scrutiny were Jason and his quest for the Golden Fleece, in which Severin constructed a 20-oar Bronze Age galley and then rowed it with a 17-person crew from Greece to Georgia in 1984 to demonstrate the journey was a distinct possibility rather than an airy legend. Ulysses and his fabled voyage from Troy to Ithaca came next. Moving from the seas to *terra firma*, Severin took to the saddle to explore the 2,500-mile Crusader route from France to the Middle East, then turned his attention farther

east to Mongolia where he roamed in the hoof marks of Genghis Khan, each time recording the expedition's adventure and findings in a book, often with a film.

He says he is compelled to explore "because it combines excitement, travel to remote places, and a series of intriguing questions to which I would like to find sensible answers, and by writing share that progression with my readers."

The curiosity has shown no sign of diminishing over the years. He returned to the seas in the 1990s in his quest for the historical roots of *Moby Dick* and *Robinson Crusoe* and sailed across the Pacific on a bamboo raft.

Already, he seems to belong to another era, more precise and painstaking, less flashy and self-promoting. He was awarded the Founder's Medal of the Royal Geographical Society in 1986 and the Livingstone Medal of the Royal Scottish Geographical Society in 1988. To these signal honours can be added a clutch of literary awards and a handful of prizes for his films. In other words, he is the complete explorer.

"For me, exploration means problem solving: that is, putting a theory to a practical test and trying to puzzle out the solution by practical experiment."

Tim Severin

Tim Severin at work on the Brendan voyage, 1976-1977.

ROBIN HANBURY-TENISON

To look at he is more silver-haired ambassador than grizzled explorer, an elegantly suited fellow who is an amusing raconteur at one of his favourite haunts, the Travellers Club in London. Yet this is no Establishment lounge lizard. Behind the polished exterior is an explorer with a passion for protecting rainforests and indigenous peoples around the world.

And though he may be spotted from time to time in St James's, he is far more likely to be out on the trail, riding horses or camels, or at home on the farm in his beloved Cornwall.

He was born in 1936 and educated at Eton, in the tradition of Sir Wilfred Thesiger, among others. Asked why he explores, he refers to the 1963 book *Under a Lilac-Bleeding Star* by the writer Lesley Blanch. "She said there was an old Bulgarian proverb that those born under a lilac-bleeding star were doomed to roam the world for ever in search of they knew not what. Must have happened to me."

Certainly, his urge to get out and about, as is the case with most of the explorers in these pages, began early. "I think I got into it like most explorers do by showing off, climbing trees and that sort of thing. All my early expeditions were just proving that I could really go farther and do things that other people hadn't done. I can remember Richard Mason and John Hemming and me at Oxford looking at maps of the world and poring over them to see what great expeditions still remained to be done and that's how Richard and I ended up making the first crossing of South America. It was the only continent that had not yet been crossed. That was all fairly silly stuff although we were given an award by the RGS for it."

This crossing of South America brought its own highly significant discovery for Hanbury-Tenison. "It began to show me two things, the first being how important the environment was. I got into the whole natural history side of life and the beginnings of what David Attenborough has done so brilliantly, which is to make everyone aware of the fragility of life on earth. More importantly for me, I met a lot of indigenous people from a lot of different places who were always very hospitable and wonderful to meet and very interesting."

He says another seminal moment came on an expedition on the upper Orinoco River in 1968 when he was made aware of the plight of indigenous peoples and realised there was something positive he could do about it. The result was Survival International, an organisation he co-founded in 1969 dedicated to the protection of the world's tribal peoples. "All the founders of Survival International were either anthropologists or travellers/explorers who had met indigenous people, received hospitality from them, seen something of their problems and cared passionately that they were totally unrepresented in their own countries, very often unaware that they had a government, and were despised by the people who were responsible for them."

Travelling on Survival International's behalf, he led a number of overseas missions through the 1970s and 1980s and into the

1990s, visiting 33 Indian tribes in 1971, the Indians of the Darien in Panama and Colombia a year later, heading an investigation into excessive logging in Sarawak in 1988 and assessing the status of the indigenous peoples of eastern Siberia in 1992 and 1994.

Hanbury-Tenison has been on more than 30 expeditions, including, as leader, the Royal Geographical Society's largest expedition, on which he took 120 scientists to study the rainforests of Sarawak in 1977/1978. The fruits of this expedition and his book *Mulu: the Rainforest* started the international concern for tropical rainforests. By 1982, such was his impact he was named by *The Sunday Times* as 'the greatest explorer of the past 20 years', an accolade he is happy to live with, describing himself as "a modest person under an immodest exterior." The titles of some of his other books indicate the enduring focus of his interest: *A Question of Survival* (1973), *A Pattern of Peoples* (1975), *The Yanomami* (1982); *Fragile Eden* (1989), *The Rainforests: a Celebration* (1989), *Save the Earth* (1991), *The Oxford Book of Exploration* (1993).

He holds the Gold Medal of the Royal Geographical Society and is an International Fellow of the Explorers Club. Unlike some of his gloomier contemporaries, Hanbury-Tenison is upbeat about the future of exploration. We are, he says, entering a golden era.

"I think we are just beginning to get a glimmering idea of how little we understand this extraordinary piece of material flying through the universe, which happens to have life on it. I mean who cares if there is life anywhere else? I don't give a damn, quite frankly. I don't care about space because it's highly unlikely I'll ever go there and I wouldn't want to. I certainly do not think it is the answer to any of our problems."

"Here we are on this miraculous construct which happens to hang together through the incredible diversity of life on Earth and we have spent most of the past couple of hundred years doing everything in our power to screw it up. Now the great era of exploration will be when we try and understand how it all works and how it all hangs together and maybe create a paradise. Odds are we won't and we will continue to screw it up, but we have the opportunity and brains and possibility of understanding it," he says.

Aside from his concern with indigenous peoples, Hanbury-Tenison is at his happiest when on horseback – or camelback – with or without his wife Louella. He says a recent journey to the middle of the Sahara "almost qualifies as being the most spiritually uplifting, exciting and emotionally charging moment you can have which is to be entirely alone... The silence of the desert and the sheer wonder of being out there with a purpose I find very exciting. It is very fulfilling."

With the photographer Victor Engelbert and the anthropologist Bruce Albert, Robin spent

nearly three months living with the Yanomami in their yano at Toototobi in Brazil.

Robin with Yanomami children, Brazil, 1981.

MARIE THARP

When you think of explorers mapping the furthest recesses of the globe, you tend to see pictures of nineteenth-century men trekking across deserts on camels, halting regularly to whip out theodolites and sextants to survey, and perhaps also to spy. You see hearty larger-than-life types with big beards hacking through jungles, or wiry thrill-seekers hiking across the great mountain ranges with trailing caravans of pack animals and porters.

What you do not think of is an immaculately coiffed woman in a high-necked white blouse and dark fitted suit.

Yet the American oceanographic cartographer Marie Tharp, though she would never admit it herself, has made more of a contribution to the field of exploration than most of those stereotypes combined. More, too, than many in this book.

The proof lies in her greatest legacy and the fruit of her life-long work, the 1977 'World Ocean Floor Panorama' map, the first time it had ever been comprehensively plotted. The satellite era has only confirmed the accuracy of Tharp and her colleagues. It is the standard map today. In the words of Mike Purdy, director of the Lamont-Doherty Earth Observatory: "The significance of Tharp's achievement and of the map's importance cannot be overstated."

How did it all begin? How did one woman attain such a remarkable feat in what was then a very male world, all but closed to women? Running through the details of her life, the answer looks like constant enterprise leavened by years of unstinting, patient application to the task in hand. Exploration, for Tharp, has been a life-long study, the polar opposite of the hastily put together adventure expedition that has become so popular today.

Tharp was born in Ypsilanti, 30 miles west of Detroit, in 1920. Her father, a soil surveyor for the Department of Agriculture's Bureau of Chemistry and Soils, set an early example. A childhood treat was to follow him as he traipsed across farmland, methodically surveying as he went.

At university she started to ponder the path ahead. "When I was an undergraduate at Ohio University I changed my major every semester and I was looking ahead at the choices of job for a girl. The choices for a girl then seemed to be for a teacher or a nurse or a secretary and I realised that I didn't want to teach, I couldn't type and I couldn't stand the sight of blood." She transferred to the University of Michigan, which was advertising for students after the Pearl Harbor attack, "saying they would guarantee jobs to girls in the petroleum geology industry because all the guys were off to war being shot up". That was Tharp's entrance to the geological world. Had it not been for the Japanese attack, Tharp says, she would never have been given the chance to study geology.

On finishing her degree, a job at an oil company failed to keep her stimulated so she returned to academe, polishing off another degree in mathematics before turning up on the doorstep of the legendary Maurice Ewing, the founder of Columbia University's Lamont-Doherty Earth Observatory. She says of that first interview with Ewing:

"You know, it was amusing. He couldn't figure out my background, this crazy woman with all these degrees – English, music, geology, math – and he was wondering what in the hell this thing could do. Finally he asked if I could draft."

She could. She was duly hired as a lowly research assistant to a graduate student called Bruce Heezen. It was the beginning of 25 years of collaboration in truly pioneering exploration of the ocean floor – Tharp was a member of Columbia University's geology research department for the next 35 years.

As men, Heezen and Ewing were able to go out on the ocean to take soundings from the observatory's research ship *Vema*. Tharp's role, though she loved fieldwork, was to interpret the data they returned with, plotting and replotting maps segment by segment, one degree of latitude by one degree of longitude. It was painstaking work. Whatever her ambitions of being out in the field, she had to wait until 1965 for her first data-collecting expedition. "Bruce took me and another girl to sea and that was the first time I got to go to sea. That was exciting and in a very small boat. I'd never been on a boat and was the only one who didn't get seasick." Notwithstanding the limitations placed upon her, Tharp was content to play her part, unassuming and modest.

"I was always quite happy to be in the background. I thought I was lucky to be part of such a talented group. We were just happy to be a team. It was very exciting in those days. We were explorers."

Tharp made a genuinely seismic discovery in 1952, shortly after finishing the compilation of six transatlantic profiles of the North Atlantic sea floor. "A deep V-shaped cleft at the crest of the Mid-Atlantic Ridge had particularly intrigued me, the position of which I plotted on a map. There it was, a line based on six points crashing down the centre of the North Atlantic parallel to the bordering continents. When I showed this to Bruce, he just groaned and said, 'It can't be. It looks too much like continental drift.' In the early 1950s this was tantamount to scientific heresy, something like being a communist during the McCarthy era."

Initially, Heezen pooh-poohed Tharp's discovery as 'girl talk'. It wasn't. Instead, it was the bedrock for the theory of plate tectonics and continental drift. It took Heezen a little under a year to be convinced. Once he was on board, it took much longer to persuade the scientific community. Together, Heezen and Tharp discovered a 40,000-mile underwater ridge of mountains girdling the globe. Critically, it was Tharp who first spotted the thin deep valley on the crest of this ridge. The rift was found to coincide almost exactly with the map of mid-ocean earthquakes.

Only in recent years has Tharp been properly honoured for her achievements. She was named one of the twentieth century's four leading cartographers and in 2001 received the first annual Lamont-Doherty Heritage award for her life's achievement as an oceanographer.

Tharp at her worktable at Lamont Geological Observatory in Palisades, New York.
She is seen with the Physiographic Diagram of the North Atlantic (1956), the six famous
profiles of the Mid-Atlantic Ridge and Rift Vally, the Physiographic Globe by Dr Bruce C.
Heezen, and samples of PDR soundings. She is holding one of the crowquill pens with
which she drew the Physiographic Diagrams of the world's oceans.
She refers to these drawings as her 'chicken scratches'.

Circa 1961

STEVE BROOKS

When Steve Brooks first conceived of making the world's first pole-to-pole helicopter flight, it is probably fair to say that ditching in the freezing waters of the Drake Passage just off Antarctica was never part of the plan. Ninety-nine times out of 100 it would have been fatal.

It was January 2003. The previous year, Brooks and fellow pilot Quentin Smith, universally known as Q in the helicopter world, had flown the Robinson 44 to the North Pole. Heading south to Alaska, they had then changed crew, with Brooks's wife Jo joining her husband for a 20,000-mile, 20-country honeymoon across America, Central America, Columbia, Venezuela, over the Amazonian rainforests and down to Argentina. Q then rejoined Brooks for the last leg.

Seven hundred feet above a frothing ocean, with 35-foot waves lashing ominously below them, the R44 gave a horrifying shudder and vibration, followed by a sudden loss of power. Ditching was an ordeal even before they touched the water. "I was watching Steve get ready to jump and thinking not yet, not yet, and he jumped," Q recalls. "I thought, that's it, he's killed himself."

Brooks, whose self-sufficiency and determination have helped build a property company which manages a commercial investment portfolio worth more than £1 billion, was not ready to throw in the towel, however unlikely their chances of survival. "I never once allowed myself to think we wouldn't get out of this alive. I know people have died in warmer water in less time than we spent in the dinghy. The difference can only be in a determination to survive. Q had a small son at home, my wife was pregnant and we just weren't ready to die."

Eventually, after ten hours battling acute seasickness, freezing temperatures, high winds, and waves that swamped them repeatedly in their dinghy, they were rescued by a Chilean icebreaker, both men suffering from severe hypothermia.

Many people would have regarded that near-death experience as a gentle indication from the Almighty that perhaps the pole-to-pole adventure was not destined to be. Not Brooks. He had a target in sight. Over Christmas 2004, he and Q rejoined each other for the last leg once again. This time they were successful. Awarded the Aircraft Owners and Pilots Association (AOPA) individual merit award of 2005, they were praised for their determination to achieve this extraordinary record. "Those of us who have more lowly ambitions in our flying lives can only marvel at the achievements of these people," said AOPA chairman George Done. "They have taken general aviation to the farthest corners of the earth, and doing so they raise all our sights."

Whatever the horrors of ditching in the Drake Passage, Brooks recalls the jaw-dropping grandeur and the camaraderie of his expedition over the white continent.

"Flying in Antarctica was the ultimate privilege, to land and walk in majestic beauty where no one had stood before, and to do it time and time again. On

Brooks says he explores because "It makes me feel alive. If you are doing something that is outside known parameters you are walking a tightrope with no safety net." His interest in exploration came from a sort of internal revelation. "One day I had the realisation that man can achieve what he 'believes' he can achieve, so I decided to test my realisation by doing something that has never been done before and discovered decision is the first step to achievement."

Brooks's travels have taken him to more than 100 countries. He has scaled Speke Glacier in the Ruwenzori Mountains of Uganda and negotiated the Zambezi white-water rapids in a kayak, none of which represented useful preparation for Ice Challenger, his first significant expedition, in 2002. The challenge was monumental: to design and then pilot a vehicle across the frozen Bering Straits, a feat that had previously eluded the finest minds of Ford, Fiat and Land Rover. Much of the challenge was technological. Could Brooks, a qualified mechanical engineer, come up with what would essentially be the world's ultimate all-terrain vehicle, capable of floating on water, motoring through crushed ice, driving on icebergs and climbing up on to them from the water?

"As the floes jostle their way through the narrow straits they crash together, throwing up pressure ridges of sheer ice several metres high which then break apart, leaving sudden drop holes that could sink the whole expedition," Brooks explained. "Add to this the threat of passing polar bears and weather conditions that can freeze human flesh in seconds and it is easy to understand why developing the right vehicle is paramount."

After a series of hiccoughs, the answer was yes. *Snowbird 6* was, unquestionably, one of the world's more outlandish vehicles, part combine harvester, part Thunderbird. It also had to be able to operate quickly enough not to be sent off course by the Bering Sea ice pack which moves north at 3mph. Move too slowly and Brooks and co-pilot would simply be swept past the Uelen Peninsula and into the Arctic Ocean.

The route in Alaska, from Nome to Wales, the departure point for the expedition proper, took Brooks and co-pilot Graham Stratford past a series of inauspicious landmarks emphasising the pitiless desolation of this extreme environment: Lost River, No Hope Pass, Heartbreak Ridge. Temperatures plummeted as low as minus 42 degrees Celsius. Technical problems abounded. Then, on 7 April 2002, Brooks and Stratford reached the Russian landmass of Big Diomedes, crossing the international dateline and entering the record books. Aside from the moment he proposed to his wife, Brooks says this was the highpoint of his time in the field, "realizing our dream to make the world's ultimate all-terrain vehicle."

Failure, he believes, is not failing so much as not getting up again. Challenges are always there to be overcome. "It is happy persistence towards your known goal that is the key to all... " He says,

"The difficult takes a long time, the impossible takes a bit longer."

"Exploration is the first step to wisdom; it is only by exploring one's expected limits that one begins to discover one's true abilities."

Steve Brooks

Snowbird 6 *became the first vehicle to power its way across the frozen Bering Straits from America to Russia, driven by Steve Brooks and Graham Stratford, 2002.*

Dame ELLEN MACARTHUR DBE

When you hear the word Dame, you invariably think of some of the grandees of British life.

On the big screen, Dames Maggie Smith and Judi Dench, in the fashion world Dame Vivienne Westwood,

the writer Dame Barbara Cartland, all women who have reached the top of their

profession after years in the trenches.

Ellen MacArthur, the diminutive sailor from Derbyshire, was made a Dame before she was 30. Honours from the Queen do not get much more remarkable than that.

Who can forget the pictures of the crowds lining the tiny French harbour of Les Sables d'Olonne in 2001 to greet the five-foot two-inches Briton at the end of the marathon Vendée Globe after 94 days at sea. Before the solo round-the-world race, few had given the 24-year-old a thought in the face of the better-known, inevitably largely male, competition. Yet MacArthur proved more than equal to the challenge, swarming up the 90-foot mast in a storm to carry out urgent repairs, gluing a sail back together for 18 hours and, as if that were not enough, replacing a broken daggerboard twice her height and almost double her weight. She overcame everything nature – and all but one of her competitors – threw at her. After leading for much of the way during three turbulent months, MacArthur announced her arrival on the world yachting stage with a brilliant second place. Captivated by the plucky young woman's achievement, a reported 200,000 came to applaud her, more than welcomed the winner. She was the youngest person, and the fastest woman, to sail solo around the world. An MBE followed soon afterwards.

Born in 1976 in Derbyshire, not the most auspicious part of Britain for a budding sailor, she remembers sailing at the age of four, an experience which imparted the love of travelling freely towards a limitless, floating horizon. Arthur Ransome also had something to do with her early discovery of the romance of the sea. The desire to explore, she says, came by itself.

"It is just inside me; I have always loved it. Ever since I was a kid I used to read **Swallows and Amazons** *books about discovering new places and camping out and finding little coves in tiny boats."*

Another seminal moment came as a 17-year-old when, shortly before her A levels, disaster struck in the form of glandular fever. She had been planning to go to university to study to become a vet but was laid up for a month. "A week before I recovered I watched a TV programme about a yacht race and although I didn't particularly think I wanted to do that race when I saw the images... I just thought, that's it, and in that second that is when I realised that it could be my life and since that moment I have not turned back. And since that second, and every day I think, gosh I am so lucky to do what I do."

In 1995, aged 18, she sailed single-handed round Britain in a dinghy and was voted British Young Sailor of the Year. Making a career out of her great love, however, was no easy task. Reading about her early struggles, one is tempted to conclude that it was harder than some of her most monumental challenges on the water. British sponsors initially proved elusive. Two thousand five hundred letters elicited just two replies and it was to France that MacArthur turned in 1997, booking a one-way crossing across the Channel to buy a small yacht and develop her career. It was in France that she learned the slang expression 'à donf' – in English 'Go for it!', as pithy an expression of her approach to life as you'll find. Her single-minded approach to going out to get what she wants, achieving it through dint of hard work and sheer persistence, also explains why she gives short shrift to whiners.

"I always find it difficult when you talk to someone and you say, 'Oh, I would actually really like to do this in the future,' or 'I'm going to swim with dolphins or film faraway places as I would really like to do that one day,' and people say that it is really hard to be able to do all that stuff and I just think that is the wrong attitude. If you want to do it, make it happen."

Her profile steadily increased in France after sailing 3,000 miles across the Atlantic in the Mini Transat solo race, a feat that won her major sponsorship. The European retailing giant Kingfisher funded her 1998 race in the Route du Rhum from France to Guadeloupe, in which she won her class. In 2002, racing *Kingfisher* for the last time, she won the same race in record time. The following two years saw her having to deal with a touch of adversity. In 2003 she had to abort her round-the-world record attempt after her mast was smashed and, a year later, she missed out on the west – east transatlantic record by just 75 minutes.

Typically, MacArthur wasted little time in overcoming this brush with mortality. In February 2005, she set a new round-the-world record, travelling 27,354 miles in 71 days, 14 hours, 18 minutes and 33 seconds, smashing the previous record by more than 32 hours. Among the many plaudits was the following message of congratulation from the Queen.

"I'm delighted to learn that you have completed your round-the-world journey in record time. Since you set sail last November, your progress has been followed by many people in Britain and throughout the world who have been impressed by your courage, skill and stamina. I send you my warmest congratulations on your remarkable and historic achievement."

For once journalists could be excused their ritual feeding frenzy of exaggeration. As one suitably overexcited commentator put it: "She is perhaps this country's greatest ever sailor – move aside Lord Nelson, Sir Francis Drake, Sir Walter Raleigh *et al.*" MacArthur would, no doubt, be horrified by the comparison.

"You have to be determined, to will your way through.
At some stage, someone will believe in you and give you a go."

Dame Ellen MacArthur

Ellen MacArthur arrives in Falmouth, Cornwall on her trimaran B&Q following her successful solo, non-stop round-
the-world record of 71 days, 14 hours, 18 minutes and 33 seconds, 8 February 2005. MacArthur beat the previous
record held by Frenchman Francis Joyon by 1 day, 8 hours, 35 minutes and 49 seconds.

DERVLA MURPHY

She is the ultimate no-nonsense, tell-it-as-it-is Irish travel writer, the woman who brought us the marvellous travelogue **Full Tilt: Ireland to India with a Bicycle,** *published in 1965. It was the first of many literary romps.*

Murphy was born in Lismore in her beloved County Waterford in 1931. A chance birthday present got her going in the travelling world. "I got a bike and an atlas for my tenth birthday; that was pretty significant. There was also a book with engravings of Norway from the 1840s that belonged to my grandfather and that used to fascinate me," she says.

> *"As an only child you are not really very sociable. I spent hours going through in winter days up in the attic in the other old house we lived in just looking at these engravings and imagining myself walking through these mountains, crossing the lake and having all sorts of wild adventures. Usually I was rescuing somebody. They were in terrible peril and I was being unbelievably gallant at least twice an afternoon risking my life saving somebody."*

The dreams about rescuing people might have been far-fetched, but the 'wild adventures' were uncannily accurate. And the vehicle on which they would be achieved had already been identified.

She says she never had any interest in school, exams or a career. Instead, she wanted to be a novelist but understood, at 30, that she didn't have the talent (one wonders what she makes of the contemporary novel). In 1962, after both of her parents had died, she decided to fulfil her childhood ambition of travelling to India. Her way. That meant cycling to Cork, taking a boat to Fishguard, cycling to Dover, boarding a boat to Calais and heading east. For six months she continued, across France, Italy, Slovenia, Yugoslavia, Bulgaria, Turkey, Iran, Afghanistan, over the roof of the world to Pakistan and India. *Full Tilt*, the first of 21 books, was the high-spirited story of her first wild adventure, including the famous incident in which she was attacked by wolves, two of which she shot dead.

"This is perhaps the moment to contradict the popular fallacy that a solitary woman who undertakes this sort of journey must be 'very courageous'," she wrote in *Full Tilt*. "Epictetus put it in a nutshell when he said, 'For it is not death or hardship that is the fearful thing, but the fear of death or hardship'. Because in general the possibility of physical danger does not frighten me, courage is not required; when a man tries to rob or assault me, or when I find myself, as darkness is falling, utterly exhausted and waist-deep in snow, then I am afraid, but in such circumstances it is the instinct of self-preservation, rather than courage, that takes over."

Murphy has a fairly strict interpretation of what it means to explore, beyond the personal sense of the word. "I do not think that word should be used at all in relation to any travelling. I suppose what it means to me is Mungo Park, for instance, setting off by himself into the middle of Africa where truly no white person had ever been. Now that's exploration, that's my favourite example. So exploration in terms of the physical and geographical, no, it hasn't been happening really for the last half century. I don't count these great scientific expeditions that go into Antarctica or wherever they go, that's not exploration really. Not with all the high-tech stuff, it takes the fun out of it."

Full Tilt was followed by a steady stream of travel books. As the years rolled by, so did the Murphy miles on the road. She was as prolific in literary terms as she was indefatigable on her bicycle, becoming one of John Murray's most successful travel writers. She was lucky, she says, to have been in time to travel as she did before the era of modern road-building ushered in a decline in untrammelled wilderness. The very titles of her books – *In Ethiopia with a Mule* (1968), *On a Shoestring to Coorg* (1976) and *Muddling Through in Madagascar* (1985), for instance – come from a more innocent, less tarmacked era.

After having a daughter, Rachel, with the then literary editor of *The Irish Times* in 1968, there was a five-year lull in Murphy's travels. When Rachel was five, she took her to India for some 'breaking in', prior to a more testing journey described in *Where the Indus is Young: A Winter in Baltistan* (1977), where temperatures fell as low as minus 40 degrees Celsius at night.

"There is the most wonderful exhilaration in almost every journey," she says, looking back on a long life of travels. Among the highlights, she picks Baltistan, the Andes, Siberia and the highlands of Ethiopia in terms of landscape, the Tibetans, the Lau and the Malagasy in terms of the people she has worked with. But it is clear that she has always been in her element whenever she is far from the madding crowds.

The future of space exploration leaves her absolutely cold. "I have absolutely no time for space," she harrumphs. "Get the world sorted out first and after that go off to Mars or Venus or whatever you fancy. But the money and the brainpower put into this while billions of people are starving and diseased, unhoused, unfed…"

She is saddened by the headlong rush into backpacker tourism, arguing that its keenest practitioners comprehensively fail to immerse themselves in the cultures through which they hurtle in a blur of Goretex and Lonely Planet guidebooks. "They are packing all of these countries into their backpack and they are collecting frontier stamps on their passport but they hardly even know the difference between China and India because they do not stay long enough anywhere to get the feel." That is something you could never accuse Murphy of.

When she is not on the move, Murphy still lives in Lismore surrounded by a family of cats and dogs. Her most recent book, *Embers of Chaos: Balkan Journeys*, was published to another fanfare of acclaim in 2003.

The cover image from Dervla's first book, Full Tilt: Ireland to India with a Bicycle, *her adventures through Persia, Pakistan and Afghanistan.*

First published 1965

OLIVER STEEDS

He is a representative of the new generation: the modern, media-savvy, high-tech, digital adventurer, sufficiently at home in the corporate and IT worlds to facilitate his career in the field. Some of the older explorers in this book would probably cringe at the words Internet and email. Oliver Steeds positively thrives on the latest technology whose power he harnesses to communicate and highlight the world of exploration to anyone who will listen.

Born in London in 1975, he went on to study politics and East Asian Studies at Newcastle University and for the first time came across Eastern culture during a year in the People's University, Beijing. His later thesis revelled in the title: 'Confucian Capitalism – The Way for a Greater China'.

He says he caught the exploring bug conventionally, through travelling. The experiences also starkly illustrated the planet's environmental challenges. "The more I travelled and experienced the world and witnessed how man is devastating not only the planet but himself, through meeting scientists, conservationists, shamans, business leaders and different peoples, it was easy to see that we still do not really understand our world or one another. I knew that the explorers had continued to push out the boundaries of our knowledge and understanding, and this has always been my driving force."

He sees exploration as a sustainable force for 'progression', arguing that we need to move on from what, for many, remains the quintessential image of the pursuit, "the colonial image of the pith-helmeted explorer conquering unknown lands and discovering exotic tribes who have known that they have been there all along!" In his early twenties he dipped his toe into the exploration

ocean, working as a consultant with a stellar list of institutions such as the Royal Geographical Society, the World Wildlife Fund and Survival International. He also embarked on a communications role, advising on expeditions, fundraising, logistics and media. At the same time he was writing assiduously for a host of magazines and journals and in the late 1990s moved into exploration proper, travelling on a dozen expeditions to China, Tibet, Syria, Yemen, Niger and Indonesia, among other countries.

He attracted a good deal of attention on his high-profile 1,400-mile expedition 'To Xanadu' along the ancient Grass Silk Road, a trade route linking the kingdoms of Genghis and Kublai Khan. Supported by the RGS, it took him and his inexperienced team – three of the group had never ridden horses before – across Mongolia and China. No wonder he popped up on the radar screen, since the grittiest details of the expedition, including being taken captive by a group of thugs, were all recorded on video and tape, allowing a real-time appreciation of the difficulties and challenges that had to be overcome. No surprise, either, that Steeds's subsequent talk in the hallowed walls of the RGS' Ondaatje Theatre was a multimedia jamboree, no mere notes and slides. As *The Sunday Times* said of one of his talks: "All the hubris of one of Benedict Allen's video diaries, but better pictures... funny, funny, funny."

The expedition also supplied him with one of his most memorable moments in the field, when he took himself off to walk and ride the last 70 miles to the Mongolian/Chinese border alone. "As I galloped across the open desert, I felt what it might have been like to be one of the Khan's horsemen galloping across the Mongolian steppe and desert delivering messages from one side of the empire to the other," he enthuses. "My research into communication seemed to make sense. I realised then that in the past 700 years, the process of communication had changed, but everything had really remained the same. Communication is still governed by the dichotomy of 'power is knowledge' and 'knowledge is power'."

In 1998, Steeds co-founded iNOMAD, an organisation that supplies services to the expedition community, together with media, business and sponsor partners, and communicates discovery. Clients include blue-chip organisations like the RGS, BBC, Channel 4, Discovery, Sony and Shell. Recent expeditions supported by iNOMAD include a conservation project in the Comoros and, in 2006, a school expedition to the Atlas Mountains of Morocco and a research mission to Kawa Karpo, a sacred mountain in Yunnan, China. He is an expedition leader and director of Digital Explorer, a programme which conceives educational expeditions for 11-18-year-olds.

Steeds, like many others profiled here, pooh-poohs the notion that we have come to the end of exploration. "We are at an age when many people are saying that the world has been explored and everything has been discovered. And yes, apart from the solar system and the oceans most of the surface of the world has been charted. But we are now moving from exploration to imploration – because whilst we have explored the outer shell of the world, we're still a long way short of understanding how the world works, and our place in it," he argues. "Today more species are being discovered than at any other period in history, and yet also more species are being destroyed than at any other period in history. If today's anything to go by, tomorrow isn't looking good."

He has subsequently worked for Raleigh International and continues to popularise exploration among children in schools, though these days most of his work is in television, which has taken him to the Far East on a series of documentaries and current affairs programmes.

He is an idealist at heart, but one with the energy and commitment to help achieve his objectives. He says,

"If we look at the future of exploration as the next great step for mankind then I believe that it has to be to find a way where our progression is sustainable, where everyone has at least basic healthcare and education, a place where global and local citizenship and responsibility can work together: a pipe-dream? Exploration begins with a dream. We all have a choice to make it possible. We can all do it. The choice is yours."

"As I galloped across the open desert, I felt what it might have been like to be one of the Khan's horsemen galloping across the Mongolian steppe and desert delivering messages from one side of the empire to the other."

Oliver Steeds

Researching the Grass Silk Road – one of the most important communication highways in history – , inking Genghis Khan's capital Karakorum with Kublai Khan's Xanadu, 1999.

Picture Credits

Acknowledgements

I would like to warmly thank the many people and friends whose support, care and dedication have been so generously given, those who have helped and inspired the creation of this book.

To Steve Brooks, my husband, for his constant encouragement and unwavering support. To Justin Marozzi for his wonderful text and insights which are so enriching to this project. To Shane and Nigel Winser of the Royal Geographical Society for their marvellous text and their belief in the project from the onset, before even I was clear of the direction it would follow. To Bruce Mitchell, my business partner, whose support and incredible eye have overseen so much of this project. To Monique whose constructive criticism and wonderful literary skills have helped the shape of this book. To Alex Sunshine for his unerring support and most importantly the light he has brought to the project. To all at Resolution Creative who have worked tirelessly on the creation of this work from the darkroom department to the designers. I think it is fair to say that everyone in the company has played a role. My thanks especially to Zain Bador for the exceptional commitment and skills he has brought to the design of this book, and to Carolina for her patient proof-reading skills.

I should also like to express my heartfelt appreciation to Alex Foley of Alex Foley & Associates Ltd whose co-operation and diligence have ensured the success of this venture. For their help in many ways, I am extremely grateful to the following: Barry Moss and Richard Weiss of the Explorers Club, Tom Sutherland of the Travellers Club, Mary Lyne Bird of the American Geographic Society, Arun Soni of Film Plus, Gray Levitt of Grays of Westminster, John Easterby, Joel Cantor, Neil Jeffers, Quentin Smith, Milbry Polk and Chris Bird. To the many at Carlton – André Deutsch for all their support. Acknowledgement lists invariably result in omissions and I wish to express my thanks to the many other people and companies who have been involved in this work but are not named here.

I would like to thank my friends and family whose love and support have been greatly appreciated, and especially my children, who have taught me so much and bring such happiness into my life. My greatest thanks must go to the 50 exceptional people included in the pages of this book who have given of their time and thoughts to make this a truly inspirational piece of work which I hope will touch all who read it. Finally, to the many more people among us who are truly inspiring but not included in this collection.

"*Whatever you can do, or dream you can, begin it.*
Boldness has genius, power, and magic in it."

Johann Wolfgang Von Goethe